Praise for
Finding Venerable

"I met Dhammananda personally decades ago and although our time together was short, the memory of her clarity and unshakable dedication and, above all her kindness, has stayed with me until now. Cindy Rasicot's loving account of her own transformation through knowing her is a joy to read."

—SYLVIA BOORSTEIN author of *Happiness is an Inside Job*

"The journey to heal the mother wound is long and dark. What a blessing it was for Cindy Rasciot to find a woman spiritual leader who shines a light upon her path to help heal her heart. Cindy reveals her courageous adventure to find compassion and forgiveness in her memoir *Finding the Venerable Mother.*"

—LINDA JOY MYERS, President National Association of Memoir Writers, author of *Journey of Memoir, Don't Call Me Mother,* and *Song of the Plains*

"A memoir of an American woman's unexpected journey toward spiritual healing in Thailand."

—*KIRKUS REVIEWS*

"Beautifully crafted, miraculously evocative, and continuously inspiring, *Finding Venerable Mother* is, at its essence, a story about an intelligent modern woman's deeply felt spiritual quest."

—JASMIN DARZNIK, PhD author of *Song of a Captive Bird* and the *New York Times* bestseller *The Good Daughter*

Finding Venerable Mother

A Daughter's Spiritual
Quest to Thailand

Cindy Rasicot

SHE WRITES PRESS

Published 2020
Printed in the United States of America
ISBN: 978-1-63152-702-9 pbk
ISBN: 978-1-63152-703-6 ebk
Library of Congress Control Number: 2019918230

For information, address:
She Writes Press
1569 Solano Ave #546
Berkeley, CA 94707

She Writes Press is a division of SparkPoint Studio, LLC.

Interior design by Tabitha Lahr

"Everything Begins Here….in our Hearts"
Venerable Dhammananda Bhikkhuni

Prologue

This is where my story began, in August of 2005. My husband, thirteen-year-old son, and I had just relocated from our home in Northern California to Bangkok, Thailand. My husband worked for a large oil company and had been transferred there for a three-year expat assignment. In the first three months, I was busy searching for housing and enrolling my son in school, but once that was done, I was in a position to choose what I wanted to do next. I considered volunteering for an organization dedicated to women's issues. Then it occurred to me that before we'd left California, I had interviewed at the Global Fund for Women located in San Francisco. They focused on a feminist agenda—helping women throughout the world. I wondered if their foundation might be funding any projects in Thailand that required volunteers. I logged into their website and, to my surprise, found an announcement for an upcoming conference in Bangkok in October, just a few weeks away, with a focus on women in developing countries. I felt a rush of excitement and a feeling of serendipity. I could network to meet other women and learn about volunteer opportunities—all for a cause I cared deeply about. The universe was offering me a gift. I signed up, convinced that a new door was opening and I was about to walk through it.

On the morning of the conference, I set the alarm for six, earlier than usual. I couldn't wait to get up. Everything felt special. The coffee tasted richer and more flavorful. I put on a favorite linen blouse and long skirt, grabbed my purse, and headed out the door.

The conference was held at the Shangri-La Hotel, a luxury five-star hotel located right on the banks of the famed Chao Praya River. My driver dropped me off at the main entrance. Walking into the lobby was like entering a huge atrium covered in skylights and decorated with lush green plants, a babbling fountain, and displays of purple orchids. The space was three stories high with individual balconies on the second and third floors that overlooked the reception area. In the center was a gorgeous bamboo tree that grew so tall it touched the ceiling. It felt like an enchanted garden. I made my way to the concierge who directed me to the second-floor ballroom. Stepping off the elevator into the hallway, I noticed the mood was quiet, with not much activity going on.

I had expected there might be, at most, three hundred women in attendance. The fact that the event was being held in a "grand ballroom" should have tipped me off, but when I walked through the conference room doors, I caught my breath in surprise, overwhelmed by the huge number of women. There must have been one thousand people, an international gathering—African, East Indian, Latina, Asian—and a sprinkling of white women here and there. Everywhere I looked, women wore native dress—bold African prints, flashes of orange and pink silk saris, Guatemalan shawls in a panorama of red, blue, yellow, and orange stripes. I had not been in a room with that many "engaged feminists" since my undergraduate studies, thirty years earlier. A roar of excitement filled the air. I glanced through the program and circled an afternoon workshop entitled, "Faith, Feminism, and the Power of Love," an unlikely combination, I mused, mixing prayer and politics.

The morning session went by quickly. After lunch, I headed to the workshop. It looked like about fifty women had showed up and were waiting for the presentation to begin. There were eight panelists—from South America, Africa, Iraq, Myanmar, Indonesia, and Thailand—seated in a half-circle facing the audience. A few of them wore earphones for translations.

The moderator led a discussion that centered on whether being a feminist or having feminist values was a contradiction with having faith or practicing one's faith. The moderator invited each panelist to speak. A quiet and diminutive woman from Bolivia, dressed in a black bowler hat and royal blue shawl, talked about her work in rural villages with poor women. I was a little sleepy after lunch and not really paying close attention until suddenly a tense debate broke out between two panelists, one from Iraq and the other from Indonesia. The woman from Iraq fired an angry comment at the Indonesian woman about how Islam was a means of oppressing women and keeping them subservient in a male-dominated religion. The Indonesian woman defended Islam as a source of personal strength and faith to poor women surviving under adverse conditions. It was like watching a hard-fought tennis match, the ball getting volleyed back and forth over the net. An uncomfortable silence followed their debate.

That's when I first heard her speak. Seated at the edge of the semicircle was a tall, slender Thai woman dressed in saffron robes and flip-flops. Her head was a fuzzy crown of black shaven hair, and she wore thin, gold, wire-rimmed glasses. She spoke in a calm, quiet voice, soothing the waves of discontent.

"We cannot solve anything by anger. Anger doesn't lead us anywhere. It is more difficult to practice compassion and loving-kindness. That is the goal of Buddhism." I woke up in a powerful flash of recognition as her words resonated deep within me. My body tingled all over, and I felt as if she were speaking directly to me. Something was happening that I couldn't explain. I simply knew that I wanted to spend time with her.

The woman who uttered these words was Venerable Dhammananda Bhikkhuni (pronounced dhamma-nanda pik-u-nee). At the end of the panel, Dhammananda invited anyone who was interested to visit her international monastery for women. Her kindness was contagious. Curious, I approached her afterwards as she sat quietly.

"I would like to come see you," I said. Dhammananda calmly pulled a business card out of her briefcase and wrote down her cell phone number.

"Come" she said, handing me her card. "Look for a large, golden, smiling Chinese Buddha seated at the temple entrance." It was as simple as that. All I had to do was ask.

That was fourteen years ago. To this day I still remember the first words she spoke, the prophetic wisdom of my spiritual teacher and healer, Dhammananda Bhikkhuni. Thus began the first encounter in my personal transformation and spiritual development.

Chapter 1:

Bangkok Bound

I was staring into the computer monitor at work when my phone rang. Even though it was not a complete surprise, my husband's question startled me. "Want to move to Bangkok?"

Three months earlier, Randall had received a job offer to go to Buenos Aires, Argentina. We'd drunk champagne on Friday to celebrate the news, but the following Monday, the offer had been rescinded.

"Is it for real this time?" I asked.

"It's definitely going to happen, and fast. I have to be in Bangkok in four weeks."

It was early July of 2005, which meant moving the first week of August. The thought of leaving so fast was over-whelming. What would we do with our house? What about our belongings? I was at the mercy of Randall's job with no say in the process. Randall was a natural-born risk-taker who often leaped ahead of me and looked back to make sure I was following. I was just the opposite: cautious, easily frightened, and slow to decide.

"How long would we live there?"

"Three years. We could travel to Vietnam, Cambodia, Singapore, and Japan. What an opportunity!" Clearly he was excited, while I felt a mixture of fear and hesitation.

Randall had worked hard this past year to advance his career. Top-performing employees were rewarded with overseas assignments. The move to Thailand meant a promotion, but it was happening so fast.

"We won't know anyone, or speak the language," I said.

"It will be an adventure," Randall replied. "This is the chance of a lifetime. I've been working for the company for twenty-four years, and this is the only foreign assignment available for someone with my qualifications. They owe me one after Argentina—and I'm not going to get another offer."

I was conflicted. I would have been more comfortable living in South America, since I spoke fluent Spanish. I'd learned Spanish during my junior year abroad living in Madrid in 1971 and felt more familiar with Latin culture. I had many Latina friends and knew I could easily blend into the local scene. I'd heard Buenos Aires was similar to a European city and I'd dreamed of leisurely afternoons sitting in cafés and sipping espresso. I could also envision our son, Kris, thirteen years old, becoming fluent in Spanish and flourishing in a Latin culture. He loved Mexican food and was already studying Spanish in school. In Thailand he would be navigating unfamiliar territory. Like me, Kris was slow to accept change, and transitions were hard for him.

"What about the cultural differences?" I asked. "I don't know anything about Thai society or customs." At fifty-four, confronting the unknown felt daunting. And there was another complication. I had a serious lower back problem that I had been coping with for the past eight years. Degenerative discs. I had grown used to carrying an ice pack and a little blow-up chair pillow wherever I went. I managed the pain with physical therapy and medication, but I was worried about the long flight. And what if my back got worse in Thailand? I trusted my doctors in the US but didn't have a clue about the Thai medical system. Where would I turn if I needed help? This might have been a concern living in Argentina too, but I would have felt more confident about navigating their health system.

"Let me think about it and call you back." I said. "I just need time." Randall's silence on the phone spoke volumes.

I swiveled my chair to the window, phone in hand. It's true that we'd been talking about living abroad for twenty years, but we had never actually done it. On our last vacation, we'd chartered a sailboat in Tonga and swum with the whales. It was all very exciting, but that had been a two-week vacation, not a long-term commitment.

I paused to consider my options. Maybe Randall could live abroad and I could stay home with Kris. But I knew that wasn't going to happen. I couldn't imagine living alone again after twenty years of marriage. When mutual friends in my folk dance group first introduced us, I was lonely and looking for a companion. An avid cyclist, sailor, and hiker, Randall was five-eleven, lean, and fit, with thinning brown hair and striking light blue eyes that gleamed when he was outdoors in nature. I was five-seven and slender. I liked my appearance—dark brown hair, hazel eyes, and angular features like a woman in a Modigliani painting. Even though Randall was seven years younger than me, just twenty-seven at the time, he seemed older and more responsible than most men I had met. He was not afraid of commitment and wanted to settle down.

Initially I was terrified to make a commitment. I wanted the intimacy but was afraid of losing myself in a relationship. Eventually I followed my heart. I loved him and wanted to be with him. After six months we moved in together, and a year later we married.

"You hate your job." Randall countered the empty conversation.

He's right about that, I thought. I was sick of my job as a nonprofit fundraiser for a mental health crisis center. I had settled into a fundraising career out of convenience, doing the same monotonous job day after day. I'd been there five years and had recently contemplated leaving. Still, I liked having the routine of working. In Thailand I wouldn't have a job because spouses of employees weren't allowed work permits. What would it be like to have nothing to do?

"If we moved to Thailand, you wouldn't have to work," Randall continued. "You could do anything you want. I'd kill for that opportunity." Looking around my office, I realized he was right. I was stuck in a dead-end job with no prospects for change on the horizon. I looked out the window. I took a deep breath and summoned my courage. Even with my doubts, I yearned for change. Maybe this was the opportunity I was looking for. I felt a rush of adrenaline, and my heart was pounding.

"Okay, let's do it," I said.

"Really?"

"Yes." I am the type of person who, once I cross the threshold of my fear, becomes very focused. It's like a light switch has been turned on, and I can see everything more clearly. Randall knew this about me. Even though I was still nervous, I wanted to live in a foreign culture. Randall and I agreed about that, but we approached our decision-making process differently. Once aligned, however, we made a formidable team. And once I made a solid commitment, I moved forward with purpose. For the first time I felt a trickle of excitement.

"It'll be fantastic!" Randall said. "You won't regret it."

"We'll need to discuss this with Kris tonight. I'm not looking forward to that."

"It'll be okay," he said.

Eager to leave my job, I walked downstairs and gave my boss two weeks' notice.

I left work that same day at about four thirty to pick our son up from middle school. Kris ran toward the car when he saw me. At five-foot-five, he had sandy brown hair, dark brown eyes, and a mischievous demeanor. Tired after our respective long days, we were both quiet. I turned into the driveway and let Kris out before pulling into the garage. He headed to his room to play on his computer. I didn't fuss at him to do his homework since I didn't want an argument before dinner. I dropped my things by the front door and headed into the kitchen.

Randall walked in at about six thirty, and I called Kris to the table. Randall and I both wore serious expressions.

"What's up?" Kris asked, observing our concerned faces.

"We have something to tell you," Randall said. "You know how I've been wanting to get a foreign assignment? Well, since Argentina fell through, they've offered me a job in Thailand. Your mom and I talked about it, and I decided to accept the offer."

"We've always wanted a chance to live abroad." I interjected. My tone was upbeat, hoping to persuade him.

"What?" Kris exclaimed. "I don't want to go. I won't know anyone." He pushed away from the table. "What about Austin? I don't want to leave my best friend."

"We can arrange for Austin to visit this summer," I said, hoping that bargaining chip would make him feel better. "We could take a vacation, and you could show him around."

Randall put his elbows down and leaned forward against the table. "You'll make new friends," he said. "It's a chance for adventure, a chance to see the world. We may not get another opportunity like this."

"So you're saying we have to go?" His voice rising. "Do I have any say in this, or are we going no matter what?"

"We've made our decision," Randall said. "We're moving in August. I know it's quick, but your mom and I are sure we can make it happen."

"You don't care about me!" Kris stood up and pushed away from the table.

"Well, that went well," I said sardonically.

Next thing I knew, Randall was knocking on Kris' bedroom door. I don't know what they talked about, but when they emerged from behind closed doors, Kris looked resigned. After all, he was our son, and like it or not, we had been talking about this for years. He had known about Argentina and probably guessed that a move was inevitable. No longer upset, he seemed quiet in his resolve. Perhaps he was taking his time to adjust to the idea.

We each took a serving of salad, bread, and cold chicken, and ate in silence.

The following week, I concentrated on finding a school for our son. The most likely choice was the International School of Bangkok (ISB), since most expat families sent their kids there. ISB began classes the first week of August, so I immediately submitted his application.

In addition to selecting a school, we had to prepare our house for rental, which meant clearing out all the furniture and the garage, a near-impossible task in just three weeks.

I thought about all my mother's things packed in boxes in the garage. She'd died five months earlier in January at age ninety, and I still wasn't ready to sift through her belongings.

"What are we going to do with all the boxes in the garage?" I asked.

"Everything will have to go into storage," Randall said. "I'll get one of those big dumpsters, and we'll toss out as much as we can."

"Just make sure you don't throw out any of my mom's stuff." Grief has its own timing, and I was still too sad to make any decisions about what to keep and what to let go of. The move simply meant I could delay the process, which was reassuring. I could always decide later.

We met with a property manager to lease our home. Randall planned to fly to Bangkok with us and stay for a month. Then he would fly home to pack up all our belongings to be transported in a shipping container. It would take about six weeks for the container to arrive.

Before I knew it, August 7 had arrived, and we headed to the San Francisco Airport for a mid-morning flight. A cloud of gray fog hovered overhead. I was both nervous and excited. The Airporter shuttle was waiting for us in the driveway. I paused to look at our house and asked Randall, "Are we sure all the doors are locked?" Randall sprinted from the van and did one final check around the house to make certain.

"All good," he replied.

We shoved our suitcases into the trunk and climbed into the back seats.

On the drive to the airport, I breathed a sigh of relief. The past month had been a marathon of attending to details, renting our home, applying to the International School, and most important of all, saying goodbye to friends. I felt as though I were moving in a waking dream. Everything happened so quickly; nothing seemed real. I just went through the motions, completing one task after another.

Now that we were actually leaving, it dawned on me: *We're moving to Thailand.* Soon I would venture into a whole new world, confronted by new sights, smells, and surroundings. I couldn't contain my excitement, a combination of nerves and adrenaline, as we sped toward the airport. For the first time in years, I was genuinely happy, grateful to Randall for all he provided and hopeful about the future. I glanced at my husband seated next to me and my son who was engrossed in his Game Boy. I loved my family. A feeling of warm appreciation swept through me. I smiled and nudged Randall on the shoulder. "Let the rumpus begin," I said, quoting a favorite line from *Where the Wild Things Are.*

Twenty-six hours later, the plane landed in Bangkok. A company driver had been assigned to meet us at the airport. He was Thai and had been given instructions to drive us to our temporary home at the Emporium Suites Hotel where we would be living the first month of our stay. I sat in the back seat staring out the window, eager to take in the scenery. The expressway was lined with tall coconut palms. Huge fronds swayed in the breeze, and bushes burst with orange blossoms. Skyscrapers towered in the distance. We drove past a curious statue with the upper body of a female torso and the lower body of a bird with two thin legs and talons. I later found out this was called a *kinnara,* a mythological creature thought to look after human beings in times of trouble or danger.

Downtown Bangkok was one huge traffic jam. Motorcycles clustered at stoplights, and cars were stacked bumper to bumper.

Sidewalks were layered in black soot. I rolled down the window of our air-conditioned car and was greeted by a steam bath. The air was dank but not as grimy as I had imagined.

At the hotel, men dressed in brown silk pants and coats and wearing white gloves opened the car doors and bowed. The receptionist offered us glasses of sparkling chilled red liquid that tasted like hibiscus tea. Hot and tired, we gulped them down. The lobby was a bit chaotic with people moving in every direction, and there was some confusion about our reservation. I was too exhausted to think and let Randall do the talking. Thankfully, the situation was resolved, and the bellboy grabbed our luggage. He motioned for us to follow him and led us to an elevator in the lobby where we climbed up to the twenty-seventh floor, and stepped into a hallway that was dark and a bit eerie. We found our room, and I shoved my key card into the slot. I opened the door to a long rectangular room, the living room, which was light, spacious, and airy.

"Welcome to the Emporium Suites, your new home," Randall said, beaming. I wandered around the apartment. To the left of the living room was a bedroom with a queen-sized bed, closet, and bath. Opposite the master suite was a smaller bedroom with two single beds and a bathroom attached. "This looks like your room," I said to Kris and motioned him to bring his suitcase in.

He immediately flopped on the bed and said, "I'm hungry. When can we eat?"

Randall called me over to the far end of the living room. Half the wall was covered with glass windows. "Look at the view." The park below was perfectly sculpted with diagonal walkways intermingled with lush tropical flowers. Tall buildings surrounded that oasis. We unpacked a few things and ventured downstairs to look for a restaurant. It was late afternoon. We left the downstairs lobby and discovered that the hotel was connected to the first floor of a large shopping mall, also called the Emporium. It was a dazzling display of bright lights, rows of shops, and noise. We discovered a food court on the sixth floor which offered Thai food, Japanese food, and even a Dairy Queen. "Let's hit that for dessert," I said smiling at Kris. He didn't respond. Maybe he was absorbed in looking at his new surroundings. Maybe he was just hungry.

We found a Thai restaurant whose menus were written in Thai with colorful photographs of plates of food. I pointed to a bowl of soup with a sunny egg floating on top. Kris ordered chicken and rice and Randall ordered a bowl of noodles. When the waitress delivered the noodles, they were topped with what appeared to be wispy insects opening and closing their tiny, paper wings. Randall picked up his fork, poking at the flapping wings, pausing before taking his first bite.

"Dad, *don't!*" Kris called out, waving his fork in the air. "It looks like bugs, and it might be alive!"

Randall stared, perplexed. The flapping died down, and it was obvious the wings were thin, dried strands of lettuce that fluttered open with the heat and moisture. We all laughed as Randall ate the "edible beast."

By the time we got back to the apartment, it was nighttime. The sooty air had been transformed into a soft netting of darkness, and blue and red lights shimmered on top of buildings in the distance. Our first phase of the journey completed, we headed off to bed. I was exhausted, too tired to think. We each retired to our bedrooms hoping for a good night's sleep.

The next morning, Monday, Randall left early for his first day at work. I barely heard the alarm. Half awake, I looked around, confused. It took me a minute to remember where I was. The apartment was pitch black, and the clock said five thirty. Randall was already in the shower. He hadn't missed a beat. We'd barely arrived, and he was headed off to his new job. He had a sturdy constitution and seemed immune to jet lag. Meanwhile, I could barely keep my eyes open and fell back to sleep.

By the time I woke the second time, the morning light had filtered in. I glanced at the clock display again; it was seven o'clock. Still tired, I dragged myself out of bed and headed for the living room windows to take in the view. In the park below, women were performing Tai Chi. Every fifteen minutes, a new group of women arrived. The first group lunged forward in sweeping dives with long silver swords. The next group held bright red fans that swirled gracefully as they twirled, swooped, and hopped through the movements. I stood there mesmerized. In that moment of calm, it dawned on me: *This could be a really fantastic experience.* Just then the apartment phone rang. It was a hotel phone with multiple extensions, and a flashing light accompanied the ring. *Who could be calling us?*

"Welcome to Bangkok," Randall said. "Just wanted to check in with you." His voice sounded chipper, his excitement palpable.

"I'm amazed we're here," I said. "Seems like we just left for the airport. I have to wake Kris soon. His interview at the International School is in two hours, and I have no idea how long it will take us to get there."

"You'd better go. Talk to you later."

I walked across the living room to Kris' bedroom and knocked on the door. No response. I heard the hum of the air conditioner going full blast. I knocked a little harder and walked in. He was fast asleep.

"Hey, buddy, you need to get up." Kris turned over in the sheets, his eyes barely open.

"Did you sleep okay?"

"Not so good. I was awake most of the night."

"Sorry to hear that," I said. "We have about forty-five minutes until the driver comes to pick us up."

Kris sat halfway up in bed, his T-shirt rumpled. He trudged into the bathroom.

"Let's have breakfast," I said, closing the door behind me.

Twenty minutes later, we took the elevator to the first level where breakfast was being served. The room was full of Asian people with a few Western families sprinkled in. The buffet was a different fare than we were used to. They served noodles and rice, dried fish, and a soupy looking porridge dish. Kris made a grimace. "I can't eat this food."

"Look over here." I pointed to steel trays heaped with scrambled eggs and bacon. "Want some?"

"I hate eggs. There's nothing here I like."

Fortunately, there was a selection of kids' cereal. Kris emptied a box of Froot Loops into a bowl, and I opted for coffee and a plate full of fresh mango, papaya, and green guava slices. After breakfast we walked down to the lobby to meet the same driver who'd picked us up at the airport. We had arranged to have him take us to ISB, located in a compound called Nichada Thani. Outside, the early morning air was warm, not blazing hot yet. When the car pulled up, Kris sat in the back seat, and I climbed into the front.

Traffic in downtown Bangkok crawled. It took about half an hour to travel ten city blocks to the expressway. I had no idea this would take so long. It was already eight thirty, and our appointment was at nine. I took a deep breath, anxious to arrive on time. Eventually we turned onto the freeway where traffic moved at a fast pace.

Exiting the highway, we turned onto a side street lined with wooden shacks and vendors selling barbecued meat cooking over an open fire. Mangy looking dogs roamed the streets.

A doctor had warned us before we left not to pet stray dogs because they might be rabid. The dogs looked thin and tired; they were pink, hairless from the heat, but didn't appear to be aggressive. The driver turned off the side street and we drove through a main gate where a sign read, "WELCOME TO NICHADA THANI, A PLANNED COMMUNITY." We drove past chalky white, two-story stucco houses lined up side by side. The immaculate green lawns reminded me of a country club. I knew the school was in the compound, but we hadn't located it yet. Security guards in beige uniforms stood at the entrance to every street and saluted us military style each time we drove by.

"Wow," I said. "This is weird."

I had never wanted to live in a "planned community," so isolated from the Thai people. Would living there be just like our home in the suburbs? I knew a lot of the employees where Randall worked lived there, especially those with school-aged kids, because of its convenient location. I promised myself if we did decide to live there that we'd get outside of Nichada on the weekends.

We drove around what appeared to be a huge man-made lake and passed a Starbucks. *How strange to have a Starbucks out here.* The driver pulled up to the front entrance of the school. I asked the guard where the main office was, and he answered in Thai, speaking to the driver. We continued straight to a row of buildings. The driver pulled up to the curb where an easel board read "WELCOME RASICOT FAMILY." I glanced at my watch: nine fifteen. I hated being late and tensed up slightly. A rush of hot air met us as we stepped out of the car and walked down the hallway to the main office. Once inside a receptionist guided us to a sofa in the waiting room. The admissions director arrived within five minutes and introduced himself.

"How was traffic?" he asked.

"Not great. Sorry we're late."

"Late is the new normal," he said with a smile. "No worries." I was reassured by his relaxed attitude. "I'll show you around first, and then we'll head over to the counselor's office for the interview." Kris and I joined him as he started the tour.

The school looked like a college campus with new buildings. "All air-conditioned," the director beamed, pointing to the classrooms. We walked past the gym and the Olympic-sized swimming pool. I had to admit this was much nicer than Kris' public school at home. We couldn't afford to send him to private school, but here the company would pay the tuition.

After the tour, we met with a counselor, a friendly woman named Sally who welcomed us and invited us into her office for an interview. I was nervous because school had already started the week before, and I had been warned that it might be difficult to get in.

Kris' gift was verbal adeptness, and he fielded all the questions with no hesitation.

"What do you think about this school?" Sally asked.

"I like it," Kris replied.

"Why don't you come in the day after tomorrow? I'll sign you up for all your classes. In the meantime, you can buy your uniform and some school supplies in the student store downstairs." I high-fived Kris after the interview and asked him, "What do you think? Do you want to go there?"

"Sure," he said. I was impressed by his confidence. He seemed relaxed, no longer unsure of where he was going.

On the ride home, I was relieved. My concern about selecting a school for Kris had just been resolved. My next task would be to start looking for a place to live. The company had paid for a month's temporary housing at the Emporium, but after that we had to move. I paused, took a deep breath, and looked out the car window at the glittering temples, my mind careening to grasp that I was actually here in Bangkok. As the car sped along the highway, my heart fluttered with hope at the prospect of new beginnings.

Kris had his first day at ISB on Wednesday of that week. The school bus picked him up at five thirty in the morning, and dropped him back home at six at night, giving me plenty of time to think about where we were going to live. On the one hand, I liked the appeal of living in Bangkok because it was a cosmopolitan city. On the other hand, I knew that living in Bangkok would mean a grueling bus schedule for our son. It was an easy choice: we'd move to Nichada Thani so that Kris could be closer to school. I balanced my concerns about living in the planned community with the realization that Nichada would be full of people like us, newly arrived expats who didn't know anyone. Perhaps it was the best location to make new friends.

Over the next two weeks, I searched for a rental with the help of a housing specialist available through Randall's work. The houses were all white, modern-looking, and primarily two-story structures. There were very few rentals available since most families had relocated before the school semester began. I managed to find one house I liked and arranged for Randall and I to take a tour our second weekend in Bangkok. The houses had names, and this one was called Maison Lan.

The house was twice as large as our 1,500-square-foot, ranch-style, suburban home in Northern California. Upstairs were three bedrooms, including a master bedroom with floor-to-ceiling glass windows and a balcony that overlooked a small pool in the backyard. The yard was enclosed by a wooden fence draped in pink, white, and yellow bougainvillea. Beyond the fence was an open field covered in tall grassy reeds and broad-leafed tropical plants. There was a perfect spot in the upstairs bedroom where I could put my writing desk and look out at the view below.

Downstairs were a small kitchen, dining room, and living room with sliding glass doors that opened up to the back patio. The kitchen had not been updated and had a tiny gas range and refrigerator that looked like they belonged in a studio apartment. The cupboards smelt musty, an old wood scent combined with stale food odors. A door on the right side of the kitchen led down to an open rectangular space with a tiny adjoining room.

"Look at this," Randall said, pointing to a small space that was slightly bigger than a large walk-in closet with a single bed and washer and dryer that practically filled the entire area. To the left of it was a tiny bathroom. I looked inside. There was an open Thai-style toilet—a hole with two footrests—in the corner and a showerhead in the center with a drain hole below it.

"Who is this for? I asked.

"It's for a live-in domestic worker."

"You mean a maid?" I asked.

"Everyone has one," he replied.

This took me by surprise. The thought of a maid conjured up the image of an indentured servant, and I felt guilty just considering the idea.

"I can't imagine anyone wanting to live in such a small space. It's positively claustrophobic," I said.

I also couldn't fathom having a stranger live in our midst. I was shy and private, especially in the mornings. I liked to have my coffee and write in my journal before I faced other people. I couldn't focus on that right now, so I set that thought aside for later. We decided to rent the house, especially since there weren't any other houses available, and this one seemed fine.

Once we made the decision to rent Maison Lan, I sprang into action again. Randall and I met at the bank near his office to draw a check for the initial payment. I had to open up accounts for gas, electricity, and Internet. The housing specialist advised me to set up each account in person at Seven Eleven rather than talking on the phone to avoid any communication issues. I took her advice, but these were time-consuming tasks. Next on my agenda was to buy beds. Our shipping container wasn't due to arrive for another month, and we needed places to sleep. I was worried about having the mattresses delivered before we moved in. Fortunately, the house was vacant a few days before we arrived, and the landlord allowed me to schedule the delivery of the beds ahead of time.

We checked out of the Emporium Suites and headed for Maison Lan on a Saturday, almost one month to the day after we had arrived in Bangkok. It had been a whirlwind, and I was proud of myself for having solved two major hurdles: finding a school and renting a house. Our new home felt a bit eerie without much furniture, and there was a slight echo to the cavernous rooms. I was looking forward to our furniture delivery. Since I didn't want to face unpacking everything on my own, I began to think about hiring help. I wanted to talk to other moms to find out more about how to go about hiring domestic help. Fortunately, the school had a lot of social activities for parents, and now that we lived close to campus, it was easy for me to be more involved.

That very first week in our new home, I attended a "meet and greet" coffee for new parents where I met another mom named Nancy. She had lived for three years in Bangkok and had recently moved to Nichada so her daughter, now a sophomore at ISB, could live closer to her friends. Nancy and I shared a lot in common. We were both Jewish, with a dry sense of humor. We were both unemployed wives of working husbands, each with a single child in school and looking to make new friends. We arranged to take an early morning walk around the lake.

The morning we met, she wore a full-length Indian skirt with a bright yellow cotton top. An artist, Nancy was short with a compact build and had cropped dark hair with flashes of silver. Her face was intriguing. She had beautiful blue eyes. When I asked her a question, she would become quiet, purse her lips together, and tilt her head slightly before weighing in with a response. At her side was an adorable dog, Mathilda, a wire-haired terrier.

On the walk, Nancy talked about her maid. "We went to the beach over the weekend and came home to find her boyfriend had stayed overnight. I could tell he'd been there because they'd eaten all our food, and I found his T-shirt in the laundry. I didn't give her permission to invite her boyfriend over. I fired her, and now I'm looking to hire someone new."

"Why do you want to replace her?" I asked. "Is it worth the trouble?"

"I had a great maid before, but she moved back to Myanmar. Her name was Tulsa. I taught her how to cook the things we liked, and she picked it up fast. She did thorough housecleaning, so I didn't have to worry about anything. And that left me with so much free time, I joined a quilting group, had time to work on my art, and started traveling with friends. Everyone here has help. It lightens your load. Try it. You'll see." Nancy's argument was persuasive, but I still had reservations.

"Don't you feel guilty having all that free time when your husband has to work?"

"Not a bit," she replied. "It's not like I didn't make sacrifices to get here. I had to leave my friends and family—all my connections behind in Connecticut. Besides, while he's at work, I manage things at home. He has his responsibilities; I have mine." Nancy's reasoning made sense, but I still had concerns.

I would have to train the maid to cook the food we liked. What if she was a terrible cook? I worried about taking responsibility for another person. And I was still wrestling with my guilty conscience over our privileged status. I wondered about salary. "How do you know how much to pay her?"

"It's standard to pay anywhere from 10,000 to 13,000 baht per month, which is about $250 to $325 a month." I was surprised it cost so little. For the same price I paid to have a house cleaner come once a week in the States, I could hire full-time help here. The wage differential seemed unfair—to be paying the same amount but getting so much more.

"Didn't you feel strange about having so much when the person you hired has so little?"

"Not really," she said. "Look at it this way, you're providing a job for someone with little education and no skills. It's a win-win for both of you. Take Tulsa. With food and rent covered, she could send more back to her family in Myanmar."

"Was it hard having a stranger in the house?" I asked.

"I got used to having her around, and there's the advantage that these houses are so big. If I want privacy I just go into my studio and shut the door. It's a balancing act, but for me it's totally worth it." I had to admit that the idea seemed more attractive, the more Nancy shared with me.

At this point we rounded the corner to Starbucks and decided to get a cup of coffee. We sat on an outside deck so Mathilda could stay with us. I asked Nancy where to advertise if I wanted to hire someone.

"There's a bulletin board outside Villa Market. Everyone posts notices there when they're looking."

I was already familiar with Villa Market. It was an overpriced supermarket that offered many expat delights including French cheeses, German sausages, and California wines, specialty items that you couldn't find in local Thai markets.

Later that evening, I thought about what Nancy had said. I was seriously thinking of hiring someone but still felt some guilt about hiring a woman less fortunate having to perform menial chores so I could go off and enjoy myself. Eventually, I rationalized my guilty conscience with the frank admission that I was a lousy housekeeper and would probably be happier if I didn't have to clean at all. And come to think of it, it was pretty great to be able to provide work for someone who could support their entire family. I felt strongly that I wanted to hire a person who came during the day and left at night rather than a live-in maid.

The next day I posted an ad on the bulletin board at Villa Market. Almost immediately my cell phone started ringing. Many women called, but their English was so poor I could hardly understand them. One woman was easy to understand and came for an interview. She was tiny at five-two, and had short brown hair, ruby lips, and a wide smile. Her body was compact with broad shoulders and strong arms and legs. She looked at me intently with soulful, dark brown eyes. Her name was Durga, and she had immigrated to Thailand from Myanmar. I instinctively trusted her.

We went inside to talk, and I found her English excellent. A thought flashed through my mind. *Maybe I could live with her.* I debated about showing her the living quarters. *Why not?* We walked through the kitchen to the compact live-in space.

"You could live here?" I asked, pointing to the tiny bedroom.

"Yes, madam, I can live here. Cheaper for me to live here than rent an outside apartment. That way I send more money back home to my family." Standing halfway up the stairs to the second-floor bedroom, Durga turned around to face me. "I don't want anyone looking over my shoulder," she said. Then she relayed a story about her previous employer.

"When I finished cleaning at three o'clock, I hear knocking at my door. Madam said, 'Go back and clean this again.' No time to rest before dinner. I work hard. Do my job. You see." I gathered she didn't want me to be overly critical of her, following her around and checking her work. In any other situation I might have been defensive, but I admired this young woman for her honesty.

Though I felt an immediate connection to Durga, I still wanted to explore my options, so I interviewed several more women. They were quiet and spoke with their heads down. Not Durga; she looked me in the eye and spoke her mind.

One week later, I called Durga and hired her as a live-in domestic on a one-month trial basis.

For the same amount of money I paid my once-a-week housekeeper back home, Durga cleaned our house and cooked six days a week, working from nine in the morning to nine at night. The wages were enough for her to support her father and younger brother.

An intelligent young woman, Durga was gifted in languages and spoke Nepalese, Burmese, Hindi, Thai, and English. When the Thai workers came to the house to fix the leaky faucet, Durga translated. She gave our Thai driver directions when I wanted to go on an errand or downtown to Bangkok. She was my eyes and ears in a country I didn't understand. She was dedicated and cared about her work, and I felt her loyalty right away.

From the very beginning, Durga and I developed a close

bond. Normally I wouldn't open up to someone so quickly, but Durga was kind and caring. One morning, about a month after she came to live with us, I was feeling lonely, thinking of my mother and missing her. I hadn't realized I had kept some of my grieving at bay in order to manage the move to Thailand. When I walked into the kitchen to get a cup of coffee, Durga sensed something was wrong. "You okay, madam?" She looked at me wide-eyed with a tender expression.

Held in the safety of her gaze, my eyes welled up and tears tumbled down my cheeks. "It's my mom," I mumbled. "She died in January."

"Oh, madam," she said. "That's why your face look sad. You miss her?"

"Yes." In truth I felt as if my armor were cracking. I had been strong through so many changes, and now it was time to let go. I looked up and saw Durga's gentle gaze.

"What about your mom?" I sniffled.

"My mom also die in January. She was sick for long time. I take care of her before she die." Durga's eyes misted up. I already knew I cared about Durga, but having lost our mothers at the same time brought us that much closer.

"Do you miss her?"

"All the time." She turned her gaze down and her lips quivered slightly. I wanted to hug her but held back.

"How old was she?"

"Fifty-six. She sick with cancer." Durga drew her breath in and straightened her shoulders.

"Do you have any brothers or sisters?" I asked.

"My older sister married and have baby. My brother only sixteen. He too young to work. My father miss my mom so much. He too sad to work. Now I earn money and send it to my father and brother."

"Is it hard for you to live so far from home?" I asked.

"Yes, but I am happy here. How about you, madam, you happy here?"

"Some days I am."

"I see madam when she suffering, and I pray for you."

I was amazed by her generosity. While I thought I was the benevolent "madam," providing food and shelter to someone less fortunate, she was focused on helping me. Durga looked up at me and smiled. "I get you more coffee. You feel better."

"Thank you, Durga." My heart swelled with affection.

She scurried to the refrigerator to get milk for my coffee and brought it to me. "Now I start to work." And with that she picked up the broom and began sweeping the hard marble floor under her bare feet.

I headed upstairs and sat down at my computer. Once again, my thoughts drifted back to my mother. I missed her, though she hadn't been an easy person to have a relationship with. My earliest memory was of her sitting in a chair, reading. I often thought she was more interested in her book than me. She ran hot and cold, quiet and withdrawn one moment, angry and upset the next. I could never predict her moods as a child, which frightened me. I yearned for her love, turning myself into a human pretzel in an attempt to please her, always looking outward to accommodate her every wish. If I just gave a little more, maybe I could be that special child my mother was looking for. My relationship with my mother was confusing; I both revered and feared her.

Katie, as her friends called her, was not the loving, motherly type. An ardent feminist, she went to law school and received a JD and then a master's degree from George Washington University in 1941 when she was twenty-seven, graduating at the top of her class. She worked in the government as an attorney before getting married and raising three children.

An independent thinker with a strong moral compass, she dedicated many volunteer hours to political and social causes.

As an adult I'd often looked back and wondered if my mother was depressed when I was born. There were no pictures of my mother holding me as an infant, unlike my sister whom she held close to her cheek with a wide grin. I remembered a black-and-white photo of me as a toddler crawling in the warm surf of the Atlantic shore. My mother looked on from the beach, staring into space, as if consumed by her own thoughts a million miles away. Perhaps her dreams of being an attorney lay buried in the sand.

By the time I was four, my older brother and sister were already in school. I started to wander in the woods behind our property. I loved taking long walks with my German Shepherd, Bonnie. There was a special place called Sand River, a dry bed with white sand. I would rest there lying on my back, dog at my side, my hand nestled in her soft fur. I liked to stare up at the clouds as they drifted by. Then I would close my eyes and press my palms against my eyelids. Flashes of light appeared before me, and I imagined sitting in a dark treasure chest of sparkling jewels.

In some ways I was similar to my mother. I suffered from bouts of depression and often felt lonely, even when surrounded by friends and family. I was never truly comfortable alone. The fear of abandonment haunted me. Suspended deep in thought, I heard a light tapping at the door.

"Madam, Nancy is downstairs." Durga said.

"Where shall we go today?" Nancy asked.

"Starbucks?" I suggested.

By this time, a month had passed since we'd first met, and we were walking on a daily basis. Afternoons we would go shopping or sightseeing in Bangkok. In the beginning I enjoyed our time together, but after a few weeks of doing the same thing, I grew tired of the routine. I wondered if Nancy felt the same way.

Once we got to Starbucks, I told Nancy I felt as if I were in some kind of rut. "It's like I'm in the movie *Groundhog Day*. I get up in the morning and have my coffee. Then Kris and Randall head out the door for school and work. I plan the evening menu with Durga so she can shop during the day. You and I go for a walk and some days into Bangkok, but soon I'm back home again. I look around, stare at the four walls, and ask myself, *What will I do now*? Do you ever feel that way?"

"All the time," Nancy commiserated. "I have plenty of DVDs on hand. When I get down, I just pull one out and watch it."

"I just wake up bummed out, sad, missing home," I said. "It's like I've lost my anchor."

"I know what you mean. The days can feel endless. There might be a class you're interested in. I'm taking photography. The weekly parent newsletter from school lists classes and events, particularly for expat moms looking for things to do. You should pick up a copy in the main office on your way home and check it out."

"Good idea," I said. We finished our coffee, and I headed over to the office. The current newsletter was sitting on the receptionist's desk. I leafed through to the last page with class listings. One looked interesting—an introductory class on Thai culture scheduled to start the following week and conveniently located on the ISB campus. I loved art and history, and this would be a good opportunity to learn about my new country. When I got home, I signed up for the six-week class.

The evening of the first class, I took a chair in the front row. The instructor talked about the history of Buddhism and the influence of Hindu deities on Thai culture. Before I knew it, the teacher had projected a slide on the screen of a woman with eight arms seated atop a huge tiger. Her name was Durga. She was similar to an androgynous goddess like Athena in Greece. No wonder Durga looked like a tank mopping the marble floors on her hands and knees, or barreling through the house with a broom. With a warrior princess for a housekeeper, I was relieved of all domestic responsibilities, which left one burning question: *What do I want to do for the next three years?*

The class was interesting, but it was just a temporary solution to my feelings of isolation. After two months, the initial honeymoon period of being in Thailand had started to fade, and a familiar gray cloud of depression began to envelop me. I should have known better. I'd thought Thailand would be one grand adventure that would keep my depression at bay, but apparently I needed more structure. I missed my close friends at home and wanted something meaningful to do. I had expected to feel great, but instead I felt strangely adrift, like an empty bottle bobbing in the ocean.

Somewhere between my former home in Northern California and Bangkok, I'd lost my internal compass. Without the familiar routine of work and friends, I encountered a void. I would wake up each morning with an aimless sense of nothing to do. Ironically, I had chosen a life with few distractions, and it was overwhelming.

I needed to find a more meaningful activity beyond a single class that I could commit to. Expat women had a variety of volunteer options open to them—helping out at an orphanage, becoming a docent at the National Museum, taking on leadership roles in school sports and extracurricular activities—but none of these interested me. I was certain about one thing: I was passionate about women's issues.

I had carried my mother's banner to fight for women's equality and developed an independent major in women's studies as an undergraduate. My interest in feminism, however, was different from my mother's. She focused on political concerns— she even named my older sister Eleanor after Eleanor Roosevelt. I had been more interested in women artists. That was the early 1970s when the second wave of the feminist movement was in full swing. I was in my early twenties and searching for my identity. I longed to discover the roots of my own creativity by exploring the lives of two famous women authors, Virginia Woolf and Anaïs Nin. I fell in love with Virginia Woolf's *A Room of One's Own* and took it to heart. I spent hours reading all of Virginia Woolf's books and Anaïs Nin's diaries, which explored her innermost thoughts, passions, and struggles to gain recognition as an artist in her own right.

In the spring of 1973, my senior year, I arranged for Anaïs Nin to come and speak at a conference. Like many students at that time, I had corresponded with her and felt she was my friend. I spent hours completing a quilt in her honor to be displayed on the day of her event. It was an homage to women artists, designed and stitched by hand.

The day I met her, she swept into the conference room draped in a floor-length black cape. A petite figure, her face appeared as fragile as a china doll and her pale complexion against the bright red lipstick shocked me. Her hair was dyed a brassy shade of red and styled in a chignon on top of her head. The multipurpose room was crammed full to capacity with young women watching Anaïs at the podium. The quilt I made rested on an easel beside her. Women leaned forward in their seats, mesmerized by the speaker, this tiny bird-like woman who spoke with a whispery French accent.

"The diary didn't begin as a diary," she said. "It began as a letter to my father. The whole thing—the letters, pictures, descriptions—was for my father. My mother said I couldn't mail the letters because they might get lost. She made me keep them, though they weren't intended to be kept as a diary. I published about half of what I've written. I often ask myself why I began to edit the diary. I was living in a lovely place in 1931, where I was a lonely writer. 1931 was also the year Henry Miller and his wife June came to visit me in Louveciennes, and that began the interesting part of my life. As soon as he appeared, I felt elated by his presence." Anaïs spoke about how, as a woman artist, she eventually broke with Miller. "I wanted to write in a personal way, very close to experience, and what I felt to be the difference between what a man has to say and a woman has to say."

After her presentation, we chatted. I was hoping she would comment on the quilt, but she didn't mention it. I told her about my senior thesis, a comparative analysis of her life and the life of Virginia Woolf. The central theme was to explore their identities as women artists and the different facets of their personalities that influenced their writing. Intrigued, Anaïs encouraged me to send her a copy, implying that she might be willing to help me publish it. At the time she was publishing anthologies of essays written by young college women, and I hoped she might choose mine for publication. I mailed it off with great excitement, assuming she would love it.

In fact, she hated it. When her letter arrived, I rushed through the first paragraph. Midway through, I flinched. Could this be true? I reread the last paragraph several times, cringing at the last line. "If you attempt to publish this, I will sue you." There was no explanation. Shocked, I crumpled the letter and threw it away. I was devastated. Inside, deeply buried, I harbored a profound sense of shame. Without realizing it at the time, Anaïs had triggered my deepest fear: I was not a good writer.

Years later, I wanted to make peace with the demon inside me, and with the woman who had so deeply influenced me as a young student. I decided to read my senior thesis again, to see if I could make any sense out of what I had written and why she might have reacted the way she did. One sentence jumped out at me immediately: "In comparison to Virginia Woolf, Anaïs may or may not be considered a great writer in the eyes of literary critics, but this was not her intention to begin with." How naïve I'd been to think that what I'd written wouldn't spark angst in my subject, much less fury. And I'd taken her reaction personally. In retrospect, I'd been young and impressionable, and despite my disappointment, I wouldn't have missed the chance to meet this enigmatic and charismatic woman. It was an exciting time in my life. I loved creating my own major and meeting Anaïs, and I was grateful for the experience.

Now I was living in Thailand and, thanks to my husband, I was once again in a position to choose what I wanted to do. I wondered if there might be organizations in Bangkok dedicated to women's causes. That's when it occurred to me to log onto the Global Fund for Women's website where I found an upcoming conference scheduled in Bangkok. Something deep inside, an invisible force—call it intuition—guided me forward that day. My hands trembled slightly as I tapped the keys of my computer. I clicked the registration box and felt a rush of excitement. I didn't know it then, but I would soon be leaving my black-and-white existence in Nichada and entering into the colorful world of the Thai people. I had taken the first step in an, as yet, unknown journey. A new adventure awaited; my story was about to unfold.

Chapter 2:

Faith, Feminism, and the Power of Love

The morning of the conference, I crossed the lobby of the Shangri-la Hotel and caught the elevator to the second-floor grand ballroom where the plenary session was about to begin. As I swung open the huge door, a blast of noise greeted me. Inside hundreds of women sat engaged in conversation, their voices bright and animated. I spotted an empty seat down the center section in the middle of a long row. I squeezed in past a woman wearing a royal blue silk sari, sat down, and glanced through the program to see what interested me. Flipping through the pages, I spotted an afternoon session called "Faith, Feminism, and the Power of Love." The notion of combining feminist attitudes with loving kindness intrigued me. I wasn't an "angry feminist" because hostility didn't suit me. During the Vietnam War protest, I'd joined a group at UC Berkeley called Folk Dancers for Peace. Dancing was a joyful way to advocate for change. Perhaps this workshop could provide me with a similar compassionate model.

The morning sessions passed quickly. Soon it was noon, and we headed downstairs for lunch. Circular tables of eight had been arranged around the room. I struck up a conversation with a woman from New York who was stopping in Bangkok for a few days. Marilyn had bright blue eyes, shoulder-length blond hair, and a captivating smile. I felt an instant connection with her. Our conversation drifted to our current lives and what had brought us to Thailand. Marilyn had an interest in world religions. Although Christian, she'd always been curious about Buddhism and decided to travel here to learn more. I told her about the afternoon session on Faith and Feminism, and she decided to join me. We located the workshop and found two seats in the center of the room. There were about thirty women in the audience and eight panelists from countries in Southeast Asia, Africa, South America, and the Middle East seated in a half-circle in front.

That's when I first heard Dhammananda speak. Unlike the other panelists, she didn't say much during the session but sat there silently taking it all in. Until the end, when she commented, "We cannot solve anything by anger. Anger doesn't lead us anywhere." Her calm voice and peaceful demeanor cast a noble silence in the room. There was a definite purpose to her presence. This tall Thai woman wearing saffron robes seemed to have an inner wisdom that captured everyone's attention. In her closing comments, she invited anyone who was interested to come visit her at her temple.

Marilyn leaned over and whispered, "I'm pretty sure that Thai woman is the same one I heard speak at a conference in New York three years ago. I'd love to visit her temple."

"So would I." We approached Dhammananda, who sat quietly packing up her few belongings in the back of the room. "We are interested in coming to stay at your temple," I said.

Dhammananda pulled a business card out of her briefcase and wrote down her cell number.

"Come visit," she said handing me the card. "Look for a large, golden smiling Chinese Buddha seated at the temple entrance." I was a little nervous approaching her but immediately felt calm and reassured by the warmth of her smile. Her eyes shone with delight. A quiver of excitement went up my spine to be in the presence of someone so spiritual, so wise, and so kind.

Marilyn only had three days in Bangkok, so we planned to leave the following day and stay overnight. Since I had a driver, I arranged the transportation. Early the next morning, I picked her up at her hotel. The temple was located about an hour's drive west of Bangkok alongside a main highway in the small city of Nakon Pathom. When we reached the main highway, a busy four-lane road with diesel trucks and a lot of noise, I looked for the large Chinese Buddha. We quickly passed through the town, missing it completely.

Nervously I dialed the number on the business card Dhammananda had given me. On the second ring she answered.

"We're lost," I said.

"Let me talk to your driver," she replied.

I handed the driver my cell phone and they spoke in Thai for a few minutes. Soon, the driver made a U-turn and crossed back over the highway. Within minutes we saw a full-bellied golden Buddha seated at the entrance to the temple. My heart was doing flip-flops, excited and nervous at the same time. Pulling into the gravelly parking lot, I noted a sign overhead that read, "Wat (Temple) Songdhammakalyani, an International Center for Women Buddhists." This was the first time I realized the temple was just for women, and I wondered if it was the only one in Thailand. Most of the temples were run by male monks who depended on women to cook and clean for them. No wonder Dhammananda had been invited to speak at the Global Fund conference. In a religious community primarily dominated by men, she was building a spiritual community for women.

A pack of barking dogs rushed up to our car. When I hesitated, a woman dressed in dark brown robes shushed them away. She was tall and heavyset and wore glasses. Like Dhammananda, her head was shaved. She smiled and introduced herself as Dhammavanna. Friendly and businesslike, she ushered us into an office to take our passport numbers.

"Follow me," she urged, leading us down a central road to a small bungalow. Walking up the steps, she unlocked the door. I'm not sure what I expected, but the room was practically bare. A fan circled aimlessly overhead, but the air was hot and stuffy. On the right-hand side was a small table with an electric pot for boiling water and some tea bags. "Here's where you sleep." Dhammavanna pointed to two chaise lounges set end to end against the back wall. There were no mattresses, just the bare wood. Just as I was beginning to wonder how my back would do on that hard surface, Dhammavanna opened the cabinet and took out two pillows and quilts that would provide some padding.

Behind the main room was a small bathroom with a sink and toilet. Beside the toilet was a pot and a twenty-gallon plastic garbage can filled with water. "You flush the toilet like this." She demonstrated by pouring a pot full of water into the chamber bowl. "All toilet paper goes in here." She pointed to a small trash can nearby. I looked around for a shower. There was none, only the trash can full of water. At least we were only staying one night. Dhammavanna turned and handed me the room key. "Now I will give you a tour of the temple."

Dhammavanna led us back to the front office. Across the road was a three-story building. "That is the main temple," Dhammavanna said. "You need to be here at five fifteen for morning chanting. Put your shoes here," she said, pointing to the rack. "After chanting we gather for alms round at the back gate." She led us across a small footbridge suspended over a pond, which led to an open field with a few trees, grass, and a pile of concrete chunks. Toward the back of the lot on the left was a locked sliding gate.

"Meet here for alms round. Wear your sandals. No talking while we're walking." I was relieved to know what Dhammavanna was talking about. We had discussed alms round in the Thai culture class. Since the Buddha's time, monks had depended on the laity for their food, shelter, and financial support. Typically, monks set out at dawn with an alms bowl, similar to a round gourd with a flat lid, and local people fill the bowl with rice. Alms round is important to the Thai people because by offering food they "make merit," which confirms their faith and builds positive karma for this life and the next. The relationship between monks and lay-people is reciprocal. In return for material support, the monks provide spiritual support and bless the people.

"You will make an offering to Dhammananda at the beginning of alms round," Dhammavanna said.

"I don't have any food," I said, anxious that I hadn't come prepared.

"Don't worry. We have food for you. And be sure to bow like this." She pressed her palms together at her chest and bowed. I recognized that gesture. It was called a "wai," and was a Thai sign of respect. Marilyn and I nodded. The thought of food made me realize how hungry I was. It was mid-afternoon, and we had missed lunch. My stomach started to grumble.

"Can you tell us if dinner is provided?" I asked.

"Nuns don't eat after lunch, but the cook will leave food out for you. I will show you now." Dhammavanna led us back across the grassy area to the front of the temple. To the right of the office was an open eating area with metal tables, plastic chairs, and a roof overhead. "Come back after five," she said. "Now you take a rest before dinner."

"Thank you," we chimed in unison. With that, Dhammavanna turned and walked away.

Marilyn and I glanced at each other. "I guess that's our cue to head back to our rooms." I checked my watch. It was four thirty, so we didn't have long to wait for dinner.

A half hour later, we headed back to the dining area. I noticed one table in the center had three bowls covered with green plastic covers. I sniffed the food. It was simple: purple rice, a watery looking soup with chunks of vegetables and tofu, and slices of raw, green mango.

"Pretty basic," I said, ladling out the soup. I assumed the food would be bland.

The rice was crunchy and popped as I chewed it. It was delicious. I sipped the soup, which was surprisingly tasty.

"I'm so glad for anything to eat," Marilyn said. "I was afraid we'd have to wait until breakfast."

I turned to Marilyn. "I wonder when we'll see Dhammananda."

"I have no idea. Seems like we're sort of left to ourselves."

I felt a little let down, as we had come all this way to see her, and she wasn't around. Whenever I was unsure, my mind leapt to the worst-case scenario.

"I bet she comes to early morning meditation," Marilyn said.

"Yeah, I'm sure you're right." We pushed our chairs away from the table. By this time the sun was beginning to set, and there was a slight evening breeze that felt cool on my face. I felt peaceful for the first time that day.

Back in our room, we talked. "Tell me more about when you saw Dhammananda." I said.

"I didn't know anything about her until I heard her speak at a conference at Harvard Divinity School on women and religion."

"What do you remember about her?"

"She was this tall, slender woman, very quiet. You didn't notice her at first. But she was one of those people, when she did speak, people listened. She had these little gems of wisdom."

"Was it anything in particular she said?"

"I remember her talking about how change is possible. At the time I was in an emotionally abusive relationship. I was afraid to leave, afraid to be alone. Dhammananda talked about overcoming fear, that the way out is possible. I couldn't help crying; I was so moved." Marilyn's eyes welled up.

"What about the guy? Did you break up with him?" I asked.

"I did. I left the conference knowing that I had to leave. And it was all because of Dhammananda." Marilyn stretched like a cat and waved her hand, fanning herself. "I'm so hot. I think I'll take a shower."

"A cold-water shower. You go first!" I laughed. A few minutes later I heard a yelp come from the back bathroom. "What is it?" I shouted.

"It's so cold!" Marilyn yelled back. She returned with a towel wrapped around her wet hair.

"My turn," I said, walking back to the shower area. I doused myself with a bucket of cold water before soaping down. "Whoa!" The cold water against my hot skin was shocking and refreshing.

Back in the main room, Marilyn was reading. I set my alarm for 4:45 a.m. It was only nine o'clock. I wasn't used to going to sleep so early, so I wrote in my journal. The sounds of the street filtered in. Car and truck engines revved down the highway. The dogs howled and barked right outside my window. Loud music poured over the temple wall. I had no idea where the sound was coming from, but the racket jangled my insides. "This should be fun trying to sleep," Marilyn said as she lay down. I spread my quilt across the hard wooden surface and lay stiffly on the padding, wide awake. My back was hurting, and it was hard to get comfortable. I checked the clock as the night wore on, watching the hour hand move slowly—one, two, three in the morning. Eventually I drifted off to sleep.

At four thirty I heard a loud thud. Marilyn was sprawled on the floor, laughing. The lounge she'd been sleeping on was divided into two sections, one side of which had snapped shut and catapulted Marilyn onto the floor. We were laughing so hard we couldn't talk. It took us a moment to catch our breath.

"Did you get any sleep?" I asked Marilyn.

"Not a bit," she sighed.

It was no use trying to go back to sleep now. We boiled water for tea and sat up talking. At 5:15 we made our way across soft wet grass to the main prayer hall in the dark. I could see the outline of two shadows moving in the distance. One was sweeping the front path to the main temple and the other was carrying a bowl of flowers. As we came closer, I could see they wore white cotton robes. Later, I learned that these women were *maejis* (pronounced maa-cheese). There were approximately one hundred thousand maejis in

Thailand, women who dress in white, live at the temple, and take on vows, but are not ordained.

I slipped off my sandals and set them on the rack before entering the prayer hall. A few maejis were already lined up. They pointed for us to stand behind them in line. I wasn't sure why we were waiting.

"*Tong-gg, tong-gg.*" A loud gong sounded outside announcing that morning meditation was about to begin. Venerable Dhammananda strode though the door, head lowered, not speaking. Gathering her saffron robes in her right hand, she took her place at the front of the line, and led the procession up two flights of narrow stairs to a prayer room.

The room had an altar with flowers in front, and behind were two or three rows of golden Buddha statues in different poses, seated and standing—all crammed into a small space. I was drawn to one standing Buddha with his right arm lifted, palm fully open. Later Dhammananda would explain that the hand gesture symbolized protection from fear. *No wonder it appealed to me.* I was the fearful type, always worrying and thinking the worst about what might happen, part of my conditioning, I supposed, from my early home life.

There were three rows of padded mats on the floor spread out evenly where women knelt to chant. Since my back bothered me regularly, I took a wicker chair set against the back wall. Two women in front stepped forward to light tall, red ceremonial candles and incense. Curls of smoke that smelled of burning wax and scented spices drifted back.

Dhammavanna and another nun dressed in brown robes knelt on mats in the front. Behind them in the second row six maejis knelt to chant, and in the third row six Thai women dressed in T-shirts sat cross-legged. Marilyn took an empty mat beside them. Dhammananda was seated to the right in a low chair with a microphone. This was the first time I had chanted in a temple, and I didn't know what to expect. Dhammananda started by singing one verse in a language I didn't understand. The women chanted their response in unison. I closed my eyes and listened as the women continued in sing-song tones. Their chant had a musical cadence and rhythm that I didn't recognize, but it was hauntingly beautiful. Sitting in the sound was like drifting down a stream, floating in the voices that pulsed through me. Every so often I would peek out to see what Dhammananda was doing. Eyes closed, she rocked gently back and forth, suspended deep in thought, mouthing the words silently as the women chanted. When the chanting finished, Dhammananda spoke into the microphone.

"Now we will do sitting meditation," she said in English, and then, I assumed, said the same thing in Thai. "Breathe in through your nose and exhale through your mouth. Focus on the breath right below your nostrils." She gave each instruction in Thai and English. I tried to meditate, but my mind was chattering, thinking of alms round. I knew I was going to give an offering to Dhammananda. *How was I supposed to do that? Would I mess up?*

After meditation Dhammananda explained the tradition of weekly alms round.

"The monks and nuns depend upon local people to feed us," she said. "Every Sunday morning people stand outside their houses from six to seven offering food, water, and flowers to the monks. Everything is prepared fresh that same morning."

"People wait for me," she said. "We bless them. The male monks just walk away when the people say their blessing, but we like it, we stay."

"I counsel sick people, older people living alone, and families where there are problems. I know their personal stories. Two women we visit today have cancer," she spoke quietly. "We say a healing blessing for them." Dhammananda then switched back to Thai. She must have given instructions because the two robed nuns and three of the maejis stood up. Dhammananda motioned to Marilyn and me to follow them to the back garden for alms round.

We grabbed our sandals and gathered silently at the gate. Dhammananda, who held a round lacquered alms bowl, slid the gate open. The two nuns followed her at a steady pace, carrying their alms bowl with downcast eyes. The maejis fell into line behind them. One maeji motioned for us to join the end of the procession behind her, and as we did, she handed one package of biscuits to Marilyn and one to me. "You give to Dhammananda," she said in broken English.

"Now?" I was sweating and anxious, confused at this point. I wanted to do everything in the right sequence, showing the appropriate respect, but wasn't sure what to do. I looked at Marilyn blankly and she looked at me and shrugged her shoulders. Fortunately, the maeji saw our confusion and took my arm. She scurried toward Dhammananda at the front, towing Marilyn and me behind.

Once we caught up, the maeji gestured for us to give the biscuits to Dhammananda. Sticky drops of sweat trickled down my neck. We managed to catch Dhammananda's attention. She stopped and turned to face us, offering the lid of her alms bowl. I froze. Dhammananda tapped the lid of her alms bowl with a slight look of impatience. We placed the biscuits where she pointed.

"Kneel," the maeji put one hand on my shoulder. We pressed our palms together, bowed, and then knelt as the nuns chanted a few simple verses. It must have been a blessing. When it was over, the maeji whispered, "Come," and guided Marilyn and me back to our place in line.

What an odd sight we make, I thought. Three nuns, three maejis, and two *farang* (foreigners) coiling like a long snake down a side street. I felt vulnerable, as if I were missing an essential part of my clothing—a skirt you can see through without a slip.

The houses beside the road were wooden shacks, stacked one against the other and open to the street with a sunshade overhead. Garbage was strewn alongside the road. There was a sour smell of decay in the air. Clearly these people were poor. *How could they afford to donate food?* I wondered.

The procession slowed before a family waiting in front of their house. A mother held a squirming young daughter in her arms. An older woman, possibly the child's grandmother, was there too. They looked calmly into Dhammananda's eyes, as if greeting a trusted friend. No words were spoken. The mother placed her daughter at Dhammananda's feet. She picked up a pot and carefully doled out two scoops of warm rice into each of the nuns' bowls. The older woman collected small plastic bags filled with vegetables in clear broth sitting on a nearby table. She placed one bag on the lid of each alms bowl. The nuns turned around and passed the bags back to us. A human receiving line, we scooped up the bags of food and handed them to a maeji who walked alongside us pushing a wooden handcart to transport the food back to the monastery. The cart began to fill up with water bottles, food, flowers, fruit, and sweet orange and pink Thai desserts.

At the next house, an old woman stood holding a tin rice pot. Her face was brown and lined with wrinkles. Eyes closed, she raised the pot to her forehead. Her lips moved silently. She picked up a cone of white lotus blossoms carefully wrapped in broad green banana leaves and placed them on the lid of Dhammananda's bowl. I remained behind Dhammananda while the nuns delivered their blessing. The words to this chant sounded different from what they had sung earlier. Dhammananda leaned in close to me and whispered, "This woman has cancer."

I appreciated knowing something about people's personal stories. Living in a gated community with other expats, I hadn't yet experienced any connection with the Thai people other than my housekeeper, who wasn't even Thai, and my driver. Walking with Dhammananda was like entering a private world, discovering a Thailand that existed beyond the locked gates of a protected compound.

Dhammananda turned down a side road onto a dirt path. Through the trees and brush, I could see a small white house with a family seated on the porch. A young man who Dhammananda told us was small for his age sat between his mother and father. He looked like a boy, but as I got closer his face appeared older. His large head dwarfed his small body. I learned later that he was thirty-five years old.

Dhammananda called everyone in close. I wondered if our group might be intimidating to the man, but our presence didn't seem to bother him. Perhaps he'd seen foreigners walking in alms round before. He glanced up at Dhammananda, a look of wonder on his face. All eyes focused on this Thai man as we circled around him. Laboring for breath, his chest lifted and fell as he wheezed in and out. He pressed his palms together as his mother lifted a precious spoonful of rice into Dhammananda's alms bowl. Filled with tenderness, Dhammananda bent over to receive the offering. We paused, watching spellbound. A wave of compassion rose in my chest. My vision blurred as warm tears slid down my cheeks. I glanced at Marilyn and saw that she was crying too. It was just a momentary flash—Buddhists, Christians, Jews, Thais, Americans, all standing together connected by an invisible thread of caring.

When my vision cleared, faces and colors came into focus. Red flowers appeared richer, pinks petals more vibrant. For the first time in Thailand, I didn't feel like a foreigner. Standing in that outdoor sanctuary, I was profoundly grateful to have found this gifted teacher who willingly accepted me, a stranger, into her community. A sense of calm flooded through me as I fell back into the silent procession, and we headed back to the temple for breakfast.

Back in the dining area, women unwrapped the food that had been donated during alms round. They buzzed around quickly, emptying the contents of plastic bags into bowls and setting the food out on two long metal tables. I surveyed the offerings, mostly fruit, at the far end: bananas and green mango, biscuits and exotic looking purple fruit that looked like small eggplants. I later learned that they are called dragon balls. There was way more food than could fit on the two tables, but the women knew what to do with the extra. Marilyn and I took our seats as the frenzy died down. Wooden chimes that dangled from the ceiling vibrated in low tones as the nuns chanted a blessing. After they finished, we chanted, and everyone ate in silence. We washed our dishes in tubs of cold water with dish soap and rinsed them. Marilyn decided to go back to our room to rest while I went to explore the back garden. Squinting in the bright sunlight, I took a sip of water and wiped the sweat from my forehead. At the far end of the garden was a tall structure that looked like an outdoor stage where a long curtain hung halfway down.

Curious, I pulled back the edge of the curtain and a flash of color caught my eye. I arched my neck and gazed up at a shining blue Buddha towering over me. Painted a rich turquoise color, he was draped in a flowing golden robe. He had long, flat ears and wide, pink lips. He sat in a full lotus position with his right palm resting on his knee, and in his left hand he held a golden bowl shaped like a large apple topped with lotus blossoms. Looking at the Buddha was like being drawn into a pool of cool, radiant light. I felt a powerful attraction to him that I couldn't explain. What was I seeing? Entranced and drawn like a magnet, I was mystified and inspired by this beautiful image. I wanted to know more about him.

I walked back toward the main temple and found Dhammananda in the front office.

"What is that blue Buddha in the garden? I asked.

"That's the Medicine Buddha," she said. "I only raise the curtain for an hour—one day a month when the moon is full. People pray to him for physical and spiritual healing." I felt chills run up my spine and thought about my back. Maybe it was no accident I'd seen the Buddha uncovered.

"He was so beautiful. I couldn't take my eyes off him."

Dhammananda sensed my interest. "Perhaps you have a physical ailment. You can pray to him. Come." She walked over to a shelf with a photograph of the Medicine Buddha and gave it to me. Then she handed me a tiny plastic card.

"This is the chant for the Medicine Buddha," she told me. "It is written in Sanskrit, an ancient language. But you don't have to speak Sanskrit, the chant is translated for you in phonetic English. Here's how you do it. Pour water into a glass. Say the verses on the card three times out loud to invoke the healing power of the Medicine Buddha. Silently frame a question in your mind and repeat it to the Buddha. Then take a sip of water."

"Thank you," I said, bowing to her.

She smiled and said, "You must chant to the Medicine Buddha. He has special healing powers for you."

Out of the corner of my eye, I saw my driver pull up into the front entrance and felt sad that it was time to go. "I am so grateful to you for inviting us to come here."

"Come back soon," Dhammananda said. "Next month

we have the full moon ceremony. Join us. We will offer chanting to the Medicine Buddha."

"I would love to." I was amazed that this distinguished nun was taking a personal interest in me.

I met Marilyn in our room where we collected our bags and headed out to the car. As we passed the office, Dhammavanna waved to us and smiled. I felt as if I were saying good-bye to an old friend, even though we had just met.

Hot and tired, the only thing I could think of was an iced latte.

"I could use a Starbucks about now," I said.

"Me too."

On the drive back to Bangkok, we stopped for coffee and talked the whole time about the incredible experience we'd shared together. I felt fortunate to have met Marilyn. She was the perfect traveling companion. When we dropped her off at her hotel, I gave her a huge hug goodbye.

"You are so lucky," she said. "You can go back anytime."

"I plan to," I replied.

I realized how happy I was. I hadn't remembered feeling this good in a long time. I pulled out the photograph of the Medicine Buddha and studied his face. "Silently frame a question in your mind and repeat it to yourself." The words echoed in my head. I asked myself, *When will I see Dhammananda again?*

Once I was back home, I thought about Dhammananda every day, knowing I would go back soon. Unfortunately, I would have to wait. In the weeks following my visit to the temple, my back pain intensified. I expected it would clear up, but unfortunately it lingered into late October. Over the next seven months, I would undergo back surgery and a period of intense recovery, during which time I would chant daily to the Medicine Buddha. The blue Buddha was like a spiritual lifeline that connected me to Dhammananda until I could see her again.

*Dhammananda receives alms from a family. The father, mother,
and son are linked together arm in arm. October 2005*

*Dhammananda blesses a woman after she has just received alms.
October 2005*

Chapter 3:

Fanning the Flames

"What's going on?" Randall asked, a look of concern on his face.

He'd woken earlier than usual, before it was light outside, and had found me downstairs in the living room watching old movies. "I couldn't sleep; too much pain."

"Is it as bad as the night we went to the emergency room?"

I flashed back to that evening eight years earlier. I'd been awake all night, propped up on all fours like a wounded animal. Randall had rushed me to the emergency room where I'd received a massive shot of some pain-numbing medication to stop the spasms in my leg. An MRI of my lumbar spine revealed that I had degenerative discs. The image of my back looked like a step ladder with plenty of room at the top but toward the bottom, it was as if the steps were stacked one on top of the other. What followed were three months of bed rest and several cortisone shots. I couldn't leave home without my blue blow-up pillow and ice pack. It was too scary to think about right now. Randall came over and put his hand on my shoulder. His worried look prompted me to respond.

"I'm okay," I said, though I wasn't being completely honest. Being in pain triggered my shame, a fear that I was inadequate. I felt too vulnerable and changed the subject. "It's only four thirty; go back to bed," I told him.

"I'm awake. I may as well make us some coffee and head into the office early." After he left for the office, I turned off the TV and walked back to the kitchen, passing the downstairs bathroom on the way. I paused to look at my reflection in the bathroom mirror—a middle-aged woman, five-seven, slender with dark hair and almond-shaped hazel eyes. I imagined myself in five years—a crumpled spine, rickety bones, and a walker. *I'm only fifty-four, too young for this,* I thought. I'd flown halfway around the world to a beautiful country, and my body was falling apart. I flashed back to one of my favorite childhood books, *Chicken Little*, whose character ran about fretting, "The sky is falling." Here I was with the sky crashing around me. My biggest fear was my back getting worse, and I didn't know what to do. My heart began to race, and panic flooded through me.

I decided to sit outside to watch the sun come up. The sunrise was reassuring, something I could count on. I inhaled deeply as the morning light streamed over the back fence. I thought about Dhammananda and the Medicine Buddha. Maybe if I prayed to the Buddha, I could find some relief. I had memorized the Sanskrit chant and repeated it three times out loud. A feeling of warmth spread through me, and I began singing "Amazing Grace." It was the one song that brought me to tears every time, a welcome release. Silently weeping, I covered my heart with my hand. Quietly I whispered, *I need help, I can't go on like this.* Around nine o'clock I called Nancy.

"Can you come over?"

"Sure, can I bring Mathilda? She needs her morning walk."

About an hour later I heard a knock on my bedroom door. Mathilda ran up and jumped on the bed.

"You look exhausted," Nancy said.

"It's hard to sleep with the nerve spasms."

"When did this start?" Nancy asked.

"Coming home from the temple."

Nancy was aware that I had back issues, but she'd never seen me look this dejected. We talked for a while, and she suggested I research spine centers in Bangkok and possible treatment options. Mathilda began sniffing around the edges of the door. "She wants to get out," Nancy said. "I better take her for a walk." She snapped the leash onto her collar and turned around to wave. "I'll call you this afternoon."

I flipped on my computer. The three major hospitals in Bangkok each had a spine center that offered a full spectrum of services including surgery. I didn't want to think about surgery since I'd already had one procedure done in the States. After that operation my surgeon warned me that if my situation were to worsen, the one option available was spinal fusion, during which the lower vertebrae would be joined together in one piece. Fusion meant the base of my spine would be frozen in place, unable to move freely. That felt like a death sentence to me. *No way,* I told myself, *there's got to be another solution.*

As I continued to research possibilities, I discovered another procedure that I'd never heard of before called Artificial Disc Replacement, or ADR. The surgery involved inserting an artificial implant in the shape of a disc into the narrowed opening of the spine—kind of like a hip replacement but in the back. The good news was that the spine could move freely with the inserts, not like in a fused state. The procedure hadn't been approved yet in the US, but in Europe doctors had been doing disc implants since the late 1980s. I discovered an

ADR forum on the Internet where former patients who had traveled to Germany wrote dramatic tales of their experience before and after surgery. "Stopped all medications, played golf in six months, no longer housebound," one read. Another enthused, "Started cross country skiing after six months." I was intrigued by their stories, and for the first time in a long time, felt hopeful that this might be a possibility for me.

I spent the next few weeks emailing back and forth with people on the forum who had undergone the surgery. Several of them had worked with a consultant who, for a fee, connected his clients with doctors in a private clinic in Munich renowned for its success in performing ADR surgery. Randall and I agreed that hiring the consultant was a good idea.

It was mid-December when I contacted the consultant, and he arranged an initial phone consultation with a surgeon named Dr. Zeegers. I made sure it was an evening appointment so Randall could join the conversation.

At six o'clock on the appointed evening, the doctor called.

"Hallo." A deep voice reverberated on the other end of the phone. "Is Cindy there?"

I cupped my hand over the receiver. "It's Doctor Zeegers!" I yelled to Randall from the bedroom. "Pick up the downstairs phone."

Dr. Zeegers had reviewed the MRI scans and thought I was a good candidate for ADR surgery. He encouraged me to fly to Germany where he could do further testing. Based on the test results, Dr. Zeegers would make a final recommendation about whether or not to proceed with surgery. If it turned out surgery was the best option, there was an opening in six weeks, early February of 2006. I promised to get back to him soon, and he agreed to hold the spot for me in case I decided to have the operation.

The Christmas season came, and we rented a small house in a tropical rainforest. Kris had gone to stay with a friend, so it was a fairly quiet week. The vacation was unremarkable. In the early mornings, I sat in a wooden rocking chair on the porch and looked out into a dense cluster of trees with thick green vines wrapped around their trunks. A familiar black cloak of depression enveloped me. A dark feeling resided like a heavy rock somewhere in my chest. The weight of my grief bore down on me.

One morning, feeling at my lowest ebb, I reached a moment of clarity. I could sit here and let my depression consume me, or I could climb out of this dark hole and get help for my back. I thought about the conversation with Dr. Zeegers and the possibility of surgery. He hadn't made any promises, but his attitude was positive. He sounded sincere and thought he could help. Something about him appealed to me. He was approachable, not domineering like other surgeons I had spoken to. I looked him up on the Internet. He was plump with a broad chest, curly brown hair, and a friendly smile. There was something about him that made me think he had a sense of humor and didn't take himself too seriously. I was comfortable with him and willing to take a chance. I felt a glimmer of hope. *I can do something about my situation.* I returned from vacation convinced that surgery was my best option. My mind was made up, but I waited to tell Randall of my decision until we got back home.

New Year's morning I was ready to have a conversation. Randall and I were sitting outside on the patio by the pool, eating fresh cold mango with hot coffee. "I have something to tell you," I said. "I want to go to Germany."

He looked alarmed. "What if the surgery doesn't work?"

"I can't stand living like this. I have to try something."

There was a finality in my voice that said, *End of conversation.* Randall knew better than to argue with me. We finished our breakfast in silence. Over the next few days, I thought about what Randall had said. Maybe he was right; perhaps I was being a little impulsive. But deep down inside, I was convinced that the risk was worth taking. Just like when I'd made the decision to move to Thailand, once I knew what I wanted I was all in. I was my own best advocate, convincing myself when I needed to be strong. *You can do this, you can do this,* I repeated to myself. I called the clinic the next day and scheduled the surgery for early February. I was willing to take a leap into the unknown.

As the date for surgery approached, I began to grow anxious. I wanted Randall to accompany me to Munich, but he was involved in a major project at work. Also, he didn't want to leave Kris alone with Durga. I understood about Kris, but the part about his work upset me. It hurt my feelings that Randall wouldn't come. I felt helpless. I wanted to convince him otherwise but didn't say anything. *What good would it do to argue?* I reasoned. *He's already made up his mind.* I just kept silent, trying to be stoic instead of asking for what I really needed.

I was committed to having the surgery, but didn't want to be alone afterwards. I knew the one person I could rely on was my older sister, Ellie. I thought about calling her because she had always been there for me. We'd shared a bedroom until I was thirteen. Ellie would talk and keep me company after the lights went out. I was not a great talker, but I appreciated my sister's chatter, like a bird chirping away at my wall of silence, constantly conversing with me. I was closer to her than to any other member of my family.

Growing up, I wanted to be like my sister; she was so

outgoing and friendly. I felt inadequate next to her. She was type A, a perfectionist, goal-driven, rational, and reasonable. By contrast I was spiritual, searching from a young age. I remember being about five or six, playing with friends in the yard, poking through the bushes and asking, "Where is God?" As time went on, I was more Ferdinand the bull, lolling in the fields, waxing philosophical on my feelings while she painted her nails and pored over *Seventeen* magazine, following the latest fashion trends. She was a top-performing student and popular—she had a boyfriend in high school. I was a decent student, a loner who loved quiet, and never even dated in high school. We looked a lot different, too. She was petite at five-three, had black curly hair, and wore a size six shoe and size four dress. I was big-boned with dark brown, straight hair. I felt like a giant next to her in my size nine and a half shoe and size eight or ten dress. Despite our differences, we confided in each other regularly. I valued her advice and talked to her often. She knew about my back problems and that I was making a decision about traveling to Germany. Once I understood Randall wasn't coming, there wasn't anyone I'd rather be with than my sister, so I called her.

"Hi, Ellie, I need a favor. Any chance you can come to Munich for a week and stay with me at the Sheraton Hotel while I recover from back surgery? I'd love it if you could." I told her that I'd stay in the clinic for four days after surgery and then transfer to the hotel for two weeks before flying home. I was trying to sound upbeat, but Ellie could hear the disappointment in my voice.

"Wow! You're brave to stay by yourself after surgery. What about Randall?" I explained about his work and Kris. "Sounds familiar," she said. She knew exactly what I meant. Her husband was similar to mine in that work was his priority.

Ever the realist, Ellie was not shy about speaking the truth, plain and simple. I appreciated her honesty, and she understood my predicament.

"Let me look at my calendar." She had two kids and needed to talk to her husband, who traveled a lot for work. She wanted to make sure that he could take care of the kids while she was away.

Meanwhile, I'd also need someone that second week to fly back to Thailand with me. I thought of Nancy, who was well aware of my situation since we talked almost every day. We had become much closer over the past few weeks. She commiserated with me and encouraged me to do what I thought was best. She knew I was going to Munich, and she was the type of person to pick up and go at a moment's notice, so I called her.

"Hi, Nancy, any chance you want to see the snowy Bavarian Alps in the middle of winter? I'll pay for your flight and hotel."

She asked if she could have a few days to sort out the logistics with her family and promised to get back to me—all of which seemed more than reasonable.

Within a couple of days, Ellie and Nancy both said they could come. By this time, it was two weeks before surgery, and all the arrangements had been made. I was resigned to the fact that Randall wasn't coming, although part of me still wished he could. It was an all too familiar scene for me. I felt abandoned like when I was a child. What I wasn't as attuned to was the quiet fury building deep inside me over the fact that, one more time, I would have to be on my own. I wished I had more support, but that wasn't to be. For now, my anger was buried deep inside, hidden away. It wouldn't be long before it would erupt.

The evening before I was scheduled to fly to Munich, I was in the upstairs bedroom packing. The air conditioner was running full blast with the door closed. Kris was out visiting a friend. I thought I heard muffled shouts coming from below and opened the door to find out what was going on.

"Fire!" Randall screamed. "In the kitchen!"

I ran downstairs to a living room filled with a thick gray haze of smoke.

Orange flames leapt from a cast iron pan on the stove. The oven hood had melted like a black icicle dripping down.

"Can I throw water on a grease fire?" I yelled.

"Not in the pan!" Randall shouted back. Clearly not thinking, he grabbed the cast iron pan and threw it upside down on the marble floor, smothering the flames and burning his hand in the process. Randall yanked the five-gallon water bottle off the dispenser and heaved water on the stove. Within thirty seconds the remaining flames were out.

"How could this happen?" I couldn't hide my exasperation.

"I put the samosas on to heat up and went outside to put my bike on the car rack. I forget about them and then saw smoke drifting out the back door. That's when I ran inside."

"Lucky the whole house didn't burn down." I was annoyed. I couldn't make sense of how Randall could be so careless, it wasn't like him. Unfortunately, it was Durga's day off. Otherwise, I imagined, she would have caught this before it spiraled out of control.

There was an uncomfortable silence as we surveyed the damage. I knew Randall felt bad, but he didn't talk about it. A look of dismay etched on his brow, Randall said, "Let's get takeout for dinner tonight."

"I guess we'll have to."

Later that evening, numbed by the day's events, I finished packing. Like the fire that erupted in the kitchen, I quelled the silent flames of resentment that simmered inside.

The next morning the driver came at five o'clock to take me to the airport. I was having coffee in the kitchen when Randall walked in to say good-bye.

"So your sister is staying with you in the hotel the week after surgery, right?" I guessed by Randall's plaintive tone that he felt guilty for not coming. Still, he wasn't willing to alter his plans in any way to accompany me. My stomach felt knotted up inside.

"It's all taken care of," I replied. My voice was chilly and distant. Randall grabbed my suitcase and carried it outside. The driver had his engine running. "See you in three weeks," I said. "Say goodbye to Kris for me. Tell him I'll miss him." We hugged briefly, and I pushed away quickly, bracing against a sudden urge to cry. I was in survival mode. *Keep looking forward,* I told myself as I slipped into the back seat. I purposely didn't turn around to wave one last time.

As we traveled down the expressway toward the airport, I let out a deep sigh. I thought about the drama from the night before and felt slightly relieved to be leaving all that behind. I said goodbye to the glittering temples as we sped by. Once I had my boarding pass in hand, I began to let go of everything—the fire and the tension. My boarding pass held the promise of healing, and for now that was all the reassurance I needed.

Chapter 4:

Munich Bound

I was not the typical tourist traveling to Munich in winter to see snow-capped Bavarian Alps, sip espresso, and eat fine pastries. Instead of gaining ten pounds from eating rich food, I would grow an inch and a half taller from two artificial discs implanted in my lower back. Radical surgery held the promise of a pain-free future.

Chilly Munich was a shock. It was already dark, and the temperature was fifteen degrees Fahrenheit. I hailed a taxi to take me from the airport to the hotel. Out the window I saw a velvet cover of white snow draping the trees, cars, and buildings. It was evening, and there wasn't much traffic. A quiet feeling settled over the streets.

My hotel room had two queen-sized beds, a bathroom, and a small table by the window. Ellie and I would be sharing a bedroom, just like when we were kids. For the first time in a long time, we would spend time together away from our husbands and kids. I was excited about that. In one more week she would be arriving.

The clock over my bed read eight, which meant it was one in the morning in Bangkok, too late to call home. I flipped through the TV channels. The Olympics were on. *Great!* I thought. *If I get bored after surgery, I can watch the ice skating.* I loved the Olympics and was glad there was continual coverage. I doubted that Thai TV would even carry the event so this was an unexpected surprise. I had one day to explore the city before meeting with my doctor. I looked through my guidebook and headed to bed early.

The next morning I caught the underground for Marienplatz. The sun had disappeared, and the sky was a dark gray haze. People were hunkered down in their coats, scarves, and hats. They cast gloomy stares into space, as if the cold had captured them and locked them inside. No one greeted me with a smile and a friendly *Sawasdee* (hello in Thai). Instead they made clucking guttural sounds, *Guten Morgan.* I wandered through Marienplatz, a huge plaza and former marketplace where for centuries, people had gathered for tournaments, proclamations, and public events.

The plaza looked so quaint. There was nothing quaint about Bangkok, whose noisy traffic, street vendors, and crowded sidewalks stood in stark contrast to this quiet, spacious square lined with specialty shops, cafés, and restaurants. People were ambling about with packages wrapped in string. Fresh bread was plentiful here in contrast to Thailand, where the main staple was rice. I was dying to find a little café where I could have an espresso and eat a pastry. I found one that looked appealing and headed inside.

As I entered the café, the rush of warm air and sweet smells enveloped me. To my right was a glass cabinet filled with *kuchen*, flat raspberry tortes, and genoise cakes layered with butter cream. I was like a small child eagerly anticipating my treat. A waitress led me to a table. The café was full of elderly ladies sipping coffee out of white china cups and engaged in polite conversation. I realized I might be the youngest woman in the room. I glanced at the menu—six laminated pages of desserts—chocolate genoise torte, dense chocolate almond torte, and hazelnut torte. A waitress dressed in a white uniform and black apron approached to take my order.

"What would you like?"

"Everything looks good. Can you make a recommendation?"

"How about the hazelnut mocha cake?" She pointed to the picture.

I nodded and asked for a caffè latte.

She brought a piece of yellow cake with five spongy layers filled with coffee-flavored hazelnut pastry crème. On top was a thin glaze of satiny chocolate frosting. Tasting the rich butter cream was worth the twelve-hour flight from Bangkok. I didn't want this transcendent experience to end and savored each mouthful, licking the last of the chocolate from the spoon when I was done. I floated out of the café still buzzing from the coffee and chocolate high.

I wandered past the square into a side street and discovered Peterskirche, St. Peter's Church, the oldest cathedral in Munich, built in the twelfth century. When I entered the cathedral, afternoon Mass was in session, so I sat down in a rear pew. I loved European cathedrals—the high walls, the rounded cupola in front, and colorful stained glass windows. As the congregation rose to pray, I clasped the rounded edge of the wooden pew in front of me and leaned against it. Worried about the surgery, I hadn't slept much in the past few days. I imagined catastrophic results. *What if Dr. Zeegers hit a nerve, and I was paralyzed? What if the artificial disc didn't hold and slipped out? What if the opening was too narrow and the doctor couldn't do the implant?* But I felt safe standing in that sea of humanity.

Caught up in the stream of voices, I closed my eyes and whispered a prayer.

Help me heal. Help me heal. Tears spilled out and my body relaxed. *Someone is listening.* I felt calm and certain I was on the right path.

I checked into the clinic the next day. Dr. Zeegers ran a couple of diagnostic tests that took all morning, one of them requiring sedation. In early afternoon, Dr. Zeegers met with me and confirmed that I was a good candidate for surgery. "Should we go over the test results with your husband?" he asked.

"Yes." This was a big decision. I felt vulnerable, in need of his support.

Dr. Zeegers placed the call. "I have your wife here. We got her stoned today."

I was still groggy from the sedative. I felt my face flush and wondered what I had blurted out in my altered state but was too embarrassed to find out.

"She's definitely a candidate for two level disc replacement with a good prognosis."

"What do you think, Randall, should I go ahead with the surgery?" I asked.

"If this gives you a chance to live pain-free again, I say go for it."

I was relieved Randall was so supportive, given his past behavior and seeming reservations. Maybe he had been convinced this was a good idea after hearing the doctor's recommendation. Or maybe he had simply changed his mind once he knew I was serious about the operation. For whatever reason, I appreciated his encouragement.

"Okay, let's do it," I said.

The next day was surgery. I was anxious about the procedure and wished I weren't alone. It was Friday and my sister
wouldn't arrive until Tuesday morning, which felt like an eternity from now. As they prepped me for the anesthetic, I checked
the time. It was ten o'clock. The next thing I knew, I woke from
surgery lying on a gurney on my back with no one around. My
body felt like a heavy weight being pulled from the depths of
the ocean. I had no idea where I was. The walls were painted a
khaki green color, like faded scrubs. The clock on the wall said
two o'clock. A nurse came in about ten minutes later.

"How are you?" she asked.

"Pretty weak."

"You lost two pints of blood. They had to give you a
transfusion."

Great, I thought. *Now I'll probably get AIDS.* Even though
that was near impossible, my mind wandered to the worst
possible outcome. Then I reminded myself, *This is an expensive
clinic; that probably wouldn't happen.*

I was wheeled into a private room and slept all night. I
hadn't realized a catheter was inserted until the next morning
when the nurse came in and removed it.

"Do you think you can walk to the bathroom?" the nurse
asked. I was surprised she wanted me to walk so soon. It had
been only twenty-four hours since surgery, and I thought I'd be
able to rest longer. I wasn't sure, but was willing to give it a try.

I rolled over and pushed myself up so my legs dangled
over the side of the bed. The bathroom was only a few steps
away, but halfway to the door I collapsed in a heap. The nurse
helped me up. She was chipper and determined to complete
the task at hand.

"It must have been the loss of blood that made you so weak."

"That and major surgery," I quipped. I shuffled toward
the bathroom sink and held on for dear life.

"I need to change your bandage," the nurse said.

I saw my scar for the first time in the bathroom mirror and gagged. A craggy line the length of the Mississippi River ran from my sternum to my pelvis. My belly button was buried in stitches of flesh, and my abdomen was swollen to twice its normal size. Fortunately, I was able to walk back to my bed without incident.

It was Saturday, and a long weekend stretched ahead. Time passed slowly. I wondered why no one was calling. I was lonely but too tired to cry. For the next twenty-four hours, I dozed and woke up every few hours. Day had turned into night. Out the window I saw sparkly white stars in the jet-black sky. Early Sunday morning, the phone woke me up. The sky was still pitch-black outside.

"Hello, sweetie. How are you?"

I recognized the voice but couldn't immediately figure out who it was. It was my sister.

"I tried calling the main number, but the switchboard was closed for the weekend," Ellie said. "I finally got through by calling the emergency person on call." This explained why I hadn't heard from Randall. "How are you?"

"Okay. There's no one around. They just come to deliver meals. I feel like I'm hidden away in a cave. Can't wait until you get here in two more days."

Hearing my sister's voice brought me out of hibernation. She was adept at getting things done and didn't give up easily. Whenever I was in a difficult situation, Ellie always managed to find me. I wasn't surprised the first call was from her.

After that I dozed off again. Surgery brought strange dreams. I dreamed of a gray-streaked cat that was howling at a life-sized doll with black hair, stiff body parts, and ice blue eyes. The cat's eyes were wide with fear. The cat disappeared, and Randall walked into the room. He began to howl and shout and wave his arms. It was a belligerent kind of yelling. Red-faced, he screamed, eyes closed in a blind rage. I appeared in the dream and moved toward him.

"Look me in the eye." I reached out for his arm.

"It's not my anger you're seeing; it's my disillusionment," Randall said.

I woke sweaty and confused, unsure what to make of the dream. Was I the cat or the doll? What did my husband mean? Disillusioned with what? I thought about our tense goodbye. I missed him. I lay in bed feeling helpless and thought about calling Randall. It hadn't occurred to me until just then that I had bought a prepaid international calling card the day before surgery. I was probably too drugged to remember. I reached over to the nightstand beside my bed and pulled the card from my purse. I stared at the endless string of numbers. It took three tries to figure out how to dial, but eventually I managed to connect.

"Hi, Ellie just called. Did you try and reach me?"

"Yeah, I just kept getting a message saying to call back Monday during clinic hours. How crazy is that? They didn't give me the number to your room. How are you?"

"Been better. I have stabbing nerve pain in my left leg and my calf muscle is in spasms. How are you?"

"Okay," he said. "Are you the only patient?"

"I don't know. The nurse comes in every few hours, but that's about it. I miss you."

"Sorry I can't be there with you. Can you watch TV?"

"CNN is the only English channel. I watch it in the middle of the night when I can't sleep."

"When does Ellie fly in?" he asked.

"Two more days." I don't remember much more of our conversation. I hung up the phone and sighed, wishing he were by my side.

By this point I could walk to the bathroom unassisted and take short walks. I wandered down the hallway and discovered another patient who I hadn't realized was there. The man was sitting up in bed. His face was drawn and pale, but his eyes were bright. His wife sat at his bedside reading. When he saw me, he smiled and waved for me to come in.

"How are you?" I asked.

"Doing great. I'm already having less pain than before surgery. I'm ready to go to the hotel tomorrow." I envied the man for doing well and for his wife there at his side. After a brief conversation, I returned to my room and lay down staring at the ceiling. Being alone was getting to me.

The morning my sister flew in, I woke early full of anticipation. I packed my suitcase first thing. Then I sat on my bed and opened the door so I could see her walking down the hallway when she arrived. Around ten o'clock my phone rang. "I'm here at the airport. Be there soon."

I squealed with excitement. "Can't wait to see you!"

About an hour later, I saw my sister walking down the hallway, pulling a rolling suitcase behind her. "I'm he-re!" she said in a singsong voice. I was thrilled. We hugged and grinned at one another. She was wearing a black cashmere sweater set, soft to the touch.

"I'm so glad. I've been counting the days," I said.

She stepped back to look at me, this petite woman with light blue eyes and dark, curly salt-and-pepper hair.

"You're so tall. How come I'm the shrimp in the family?" Ellie said. "I've always wanted to be taller; you're lucky." After years of feeling inadequate in comparison to her, it was nice to hear that she admired me too. I was so happy to see my sister.

I called the nurse down the hall to join us. When she arrived I asked, "Is there anything else, or can I check out?"

"Just sign these papers and you're discharged."

We hailed a taxi and traveled two blocks to the Sheraton. While we waited in the room for our luggage, Ellie plugged in her laptop. "I have to call Peter and remind him he has a history paper due and he needs to sign up for the SAT. I have to remind him of everything."

I marveled at my sister. She'd hardly had a chance to catch her breath, and already she was phoning home to check in on her son. Deep down inside, my sister and I were alike, consummate worriers. Perhaps that was something we'd inherited from our Jewish parents. Fear had been a big part of our upbringing. My mother always warned us to be careful and admonished us to do the right thing, as if there were some critical standard of perfection to adhere to. In any case, I never felt I measured up to my mother's unrealistically high expectations.

"Let's celebrate," I said. "How about dinner in the hotel tonight?"

"Sounds good."

The next morning we decided to explore together. Beyond the hotel doors was an open cobblestone plaza lined with shops and restaurants. The plaza was clear of snow and the sun was out.

"I need to get a prescription filled at the pharmacy. It's close by."

The pharmacy was filled with expensive face creams and homeopathic remedies. "I'm still taking the same old medications," I explained to my sister as I took the bag off the counter. "Vicodin, Celebrex, and Neurontin—the full cocktail. It's depressing." I'd hoped to be off all medications after surgery.

"How long does the doctor think you'll be on the medication?"

"He doesn't know."

We found an Italian restaurant and ate lunch. Then I was tired since I hadn't stayed up this long for the past few days, so we returned to our room. I lay down for an afternoon rest while my sister worked on her computer. When I woke up, it was late afternoon, and the sky had turned a dark gray. We decided to explore some more and found a café for a cup of coffee. I couldn't resist a piece of warm apple strudel.

"Want some?" I asked, offering a spoonful to my sister.

"No thanks. I don't want to spoil my appetite for dinner." A twinge of guilt came over me as I savored the tart apples and sweet pastry shell. Ellie was unshaken in her conviction to consume tiny amounts of food. As I dusted the last crumbs off my lap, a familiar feeling of inadequacy came over me, like she was strong and I was weak. I was breaking a cardinal family rule: "Don't enjoy yourself too much; you'll only have to pay for it afterwards." Still, as we headed out of the café and afternoon light turned to dusk, I felt a huge sense of relief, grateful for her company. It didn't matter to me what we did, so long as we did it together.

That night as we got ready for bed, we started to giggle, just like when we were little. One of my hidden talents was that I could make my sister laugh hysterically until she gasped and snorted. I don't remember what I did to inspire this episode, but it was fun to let go in a fit of laughter. We both heaved slowly to catch our breath.

Once we settled down for the night, Ellie was about to turn off the lamp over her bed, but instead got up and turned on the bathroom light. "I can't go to sleep unless I leave the light on," she confessed.

"I'm the same way. I can't get to sleep without a night-light. Do you wake up during the night and have a hard time getting back to sleep?"

"All the time. I'm a very light sleeper."

"Hope I don't wake you up," I said. "I toss and turn a lot."

"Don't worry about it. We'll do the best we can." Ellie rolled over and tucked the sheet around her shoulders.

"Thanks for coming." A tiny giggle bubbled up in me. "We're still the silliest when we're together."

"I know, we can't help ourselves," she giggled back. "Sleep well. See you in the morning."

The next morning we took the elevator down to the first floor for breakfast. There were four stations: an omelet table with a chef standing waiting to take special orders; a long table with every imaginable kind of cheese, cold cuts, and salads; an area for cold cereal and dried fruits and nuts; and another station for tea and coffee. In addition to eggs, there were trays of hot sausages, bacon, fresh pancakes, and French toast.

"Breakfast and lunch in one meal," I said with a smile. I ladled out a bowl of white, creamy yogurt and piled fresh fruit and granola on top. I was so thrilled to be in a Western country; none of this food was available in Thailand. Most likely a Thai breakfast would consist of rice congee porridge, wide noodles in soy sauce, teeny dried fish, and other delicacies.

"This rye bread is unbelievably good. I'm going to make a sandwich and wrap it up for later," Ellie exclaimed as she munched on a hard green dill pickle.

The morning sunlight cast a dim shadow on the breakfast room; the windows were streaked with dusty brown snow that had caked up in a previous snowstorm. "Let's go explore the university area today."

"Fine with me," Ellie replied.

We wrapped up in our heavy coats and woolen scarves and left the warmth of the hotel to walk outside onto the back plaza and into the U-Bahn. We got off the train after three stops, passing by sand-colored brick buildings with elaborate archways.

Ellie translated the names into English. "School of Biology," she announced. We walked down a long block past the School of Philosophy, and the School of History. A couple of blocks past the university were restaurants and small shops. We stumbled upon a small clothing boutique and went inside.

"*Buon giorno.*" A man with a slightly balding head came out from the rear of the shop. Ellie was looking at the shoe display and picked out a pair of low-heeled walking shoes, caramel-colored and made of fine Italian leather.

"These would be great for touring the city," she observed.

"Do you see them in a larger size?" I asked.

Ellie surveyed the shelf. "No, just thirty-seven, must be a sample size."

I looked through the dress rack. I hadn't bought a dress in years and wasn't much interested, but at the far end of the store was a rack of leather jackets all marked down 50 percent.

I spotted a purple leather jacket. It was short, just down to my waist, with a lot of zippers, resembling a World War II bomber's jacket but way more stylish. "Look at this!" I said. Ellie encouraged me to try it on, and it fit me like a glove. I calculated the difference between euros and dollars. "It's three hundred fifty dollars."

"That's a lot of money," Ellie said, "but it looks great on you."

I traced the soft leather with my fingers and examined the label. *Just Cavalli,* it said. I'd never owned a designer label.

I felt that old adrenaline rush, pure shopping greed. But I was hooked.

"It's a bargain," the salesman remarked. "You won't find that jacket at that price anywhere, not even Italy."

"Are you sure you'll wear it?" Ellie cautioned.

"I may not wear it now, but when we go back to the States, I will. This is not a practical purchase, but it's my heart's desire." A feeling of joy surged through me. I didn't care what the jacket cost or that my sister thought it was extravagant. I'd come to Germany on my own and made it through major surgery. I was in the mood to celebrate. "I deserve this, and I'm buying it," I said, placing my credit card on the counter. In one quick swipe the deed was done.

Ellie, always the practical one, picked out a white cashmere cardigan and tried on a black trench coat, a classic design.

"Will you take our picture?" I asked the salesman. We posed beside a faceless mannequin dressed in a pink-sequined dress.

"How's this?" The salesman displayed the image.

We both wore huge grins: me in my purple leather jacket, Ellie in her new cashmere sweater, the mannequin in between us. Years from then, every time I'd look at that purple jacket, I'd smile. It would forever remind me of that perfect day in Munich with my sister.

The glow of spending time together continued for the rest of the week. I was so elated to be out of the hospital that I walked to the clinic for physical therapy in the morning and continued walking as we explored the city. It was a lot of activity given what my body had been through. In the afternoons I would take long naps. But as my time with my sister grew to a close, my frustration mounted. I missed Randall and was annoyed at the amount of pain I was still feeling. I talked to other patients living at the hotel who said they had felt instant relief after surgery. Instead of feeling better, my sciatica was worse. I couldn't sit for more than ten minutes at a time. Going to a restaurant was like being on a seesaw. I would sit for a while, stand for a few minutes, and then sit down again. I was frustrated with my level of discomfort.

The truth was I still resented Randall for not coming with me and held onto it like an old friend. Underneath the anger, my pain lay buried. I held onto the bitterness, unable to let go or acknowledge the disappointment I felt. The surgery was intended to help me, but the injustice of being sliced into like a Sunday rib roast and tied together with stitches made me livid. Being strong had always gotten me through, but the walls were crumbling and my emotions were tipping from one extreme to the other.

One afternoon in particular was hard. My sister had gone out for a while. In just two days she would be leaving, and I was already dreading saying goodbye. I started to obsess about Randall not coming to Munich with me. *How could he abandon me like that?* I could not get this thought out of my head even though part of me felt ridiculous. *What if I called him?* I picked up the phone and dialed home.

"How come you didn't come to Munich?" I blurted.

"What brought this on?" Randall snapped. "We've already had this conversation."

"Why are we even married? You don't even care about me!"

"You're just being dramatic; of course I care about you."

"If you loved me, you wouldn't have abandoned me!" Even as the words escaped my lips, I couldn't believe I was saying them.

"You're just trying to make me feel guilty," he said and hung up.

My blood was boiling, which was strangely comforting,

but like a landslide that had given way, I started to cry. Not a few tears, but huge choking and moaning sounds. I felt alone, exhausted, and defeated. I lay down, covered my head with a pillow, and fell asleep.

When I woke up, I thought about Dhammananda, sitting in her calm presence, carefully tracing the wise woman's face. I imagined kneeling before her. She would extend her hand over my head as she chanted. I tucked the memory inside my heart and returned to it again and again. Visualizing Dhammananda held the promise of healing, and I was determined to see her as soon as possible.

By the time Ellie returned to our room, I felt calmer.

"Where'd you go? I asked.

"Took a long walk and grabbed a cup of coffee. I found an Italian place that looks good, not too far, across the plaza."

An hour later we headed for the restaurant Ellie had found. Outside, the cold, fresh air flushed through my lungs as I took my sister's arm, grateful for her company.

When Nancy showed up the following day, the countdown was on for Ellie's departure. I was happy to see my friend but felt sorrow creeping up on me. I hadn't seen my sister for at least a year, and living in Thailand meant I couldn't be sure when I'd see her again. On the day we said our goodbyes, I brushed away a tear. I reached out to embrace her and we hugged.

The entire next week, Nancy and I toured the city and shopped. We enjoyed each other's company, but by week's end I was beyond ready to go home. I had spent almost three weeks in Munich and was missing my family. On top of that, I was discouraged that I was still in so much pain. I even questioned whether the whole surgery had been a mistake. I just wanted to be in familiar surroundings where I could relax and not worry about where I would go for my next meal—and to sleep in my own bed. For that to happen I knew there was one more hurdle to face: the dreaded flight home to Thailand.

I knew it would be uncomfortable sitting for ten hours in a business class seat, so I upgraded my ticket to first class where I could lie down flat. The last morning in Munich, Nancy and I bundled up one last time and caught a taxi to the airport. All I could think about was seeing Randall and Kris and hugging them tight. I was tired of the fine pastries, shopping, and cold weather. I wanted to feel the heat of Bangkok, the steamy air and the sweat dripping down my face. I would have never imagined four months ago that I'd harbor this deep feeling of longing to set foot on Thai soil.

Chapter 5:

Recovery

Back home in Bangkok, I faced an intense period of recovery. It would be three full months before I'd feel well enough to resume my normal activities. During that time, Durga took care of the family because I wasn't able to. She tended to my every need as I wandered from room to room like a wounded bird seeking shelter. Healing has its own timetable and required patience, something I lacked.

The days progressed slowly. I woke at five o'clock to the sound of Muslim chants in the distance. Dogs barked and birds chirped, alerting me to the coming dawn. Randall and Kris left the house early. The minutes ticked by like a slow-leaking faucet, drip by drip. Nancy visited often, and I had the help of a physical therapist, the only rehabilitation therapist in Bangkok who made home visits, but my progress was slow. I was frustrated that I wasn't feeling better. The physical therapist explained that invasive surgery causes inflammation. He reassured me I would get better, but it would take longer than I had expected. Once again I needed help. I turned to the Medicine Buddha and sought refuge in his healing presence.

Every day I practiced the same ritual. I would take the picture of the Medicine Buddha from my nightstand and whisper the chant I had learned. With each breath I inhaled his healing energy. I felt a warm glow as I basked in his embrace. In my mind's eye, I imagined the Buddha's outstretched hand leading me forward step by step on a healing path. Chanting to the Medicine Buddha gave me a sense of hope to endure the slow trajectory of my recovery.

Meanwhile, as my healing progressed, Randall and Kris left on spring break to stay at an exclusive beach resort called the Pimalai on an island on the southern Gulf Coast of Thailand. I had planned the trip in January and thought, for sure, by mid-April I would be able to join them. Unfortunately, I wasn't ready to travel. The day they left, part of me was relieved, but part of me was desperate to go with them. I had a familiar sinking feeling; here I was, alone again and missing my family. What I really wanted was to hop in the car and travel down to the temple, but I couldn't manage to sit for the hour-and-a-half drive just yet. Fortunately, I had Durga to take care of me. She had become my lifeline. I was also grateful to Nancy, my ever-faithful friend whose frequent visits helped to alleviate my loneliness. It was a miserable three months while I was recovering, but thanks to Durga and Nancy, I managed to survive it.

By the time my birthday came in early May, I was feeling better. Nancy and I planned a special lunch by the Chao Phraya River to celebrate. The cool breeze from the river provided relief from the hot midday sun. As we talked, I brought up the subject of Dhammananda and how much I wanted to see her but couldn't manage the long drive. Nancy looked up from her soup bowl.

"I heard she's giving three lectures on Buddhism as part of the docent training at the National Museum," she said.

"When?"

"End of May."

"I bet I can do that," I said. "The museum is only a half hour away. I can sit near the back and stand during the lecture if I need to." I was excited. I had been thinking of writing an article about Dhammananda for a local American women's magazine, and this would be a perfect opportunity to ask her for an interview. I imagined walking into the room. We would greet one another like old friends, and Dhammananda would reach for my hand.

The image of reuniting with Dhammananda stayed with me until the day of the lecture. I arrived ten minutes early and took a seat at the back of the room so I could stand if necessary. The room was full of fifty or so expat women. Dhammananda was busy setting up her computer in the front of the room. *Better to wait until the break to talk to her,* I thought.

Dhammananda stood up and began to speak. Her eyes were bright and her smile infectious. "Allow me to start by chanting; that is my profession." She pressed her palms together, sang a few verses, and then stopped.

"This chant is about the first ordained woman." she said. "Maha Pajapati Gotami Theri was the first *bhikkhuni*, the very first fully ordained nun in the Buddha's time. She was the Buddha's aunt and stepmother."

"Why do I start with this chant?" She leaned forward earnestly. "The fact that I am standing here is because of her; she is my spiritual root. I was most impressed with the Buddha's words when he accepted women to be ordained because he said, 'Women can be enlightened. They can see it with their own eyes.' This was the golden phrase," she pointed out emphatically, "the reason he allowed hundreds of women to be ordained."

"I always say that the Buddha was the first feminist. He was the first one in world religions to acknowledge that men and women are equal spiritually. No one has the right to stop what was given to us. That is my strength." Dhammananda spoke quietly but with such clarity of conviction. Her gentle outer demeanor belied an inner sense of determination and fearlessness. I was impressed that she could be both vulnerable and strong at the same time. The only other powerful woman I knew was my mother, and she was just the opposite of Dhammananda—controlling, domineering, and critical. I never felt safe with my mom, because she was neither soft nor forgiving. Dhammananda was introducing me to a new paradigm of what it meant to be feminine and empowered. I trusted her implicitly.

"You are looking at a rare species because in Thailand I am the first fully ordained Theravadin bhikkhuni. I went to Sri Lanka to be ordained because Thailand does not allow ordination of women. My mother, Venerable Voramai, was ordained before me, but in a different branch of Buddhism, the Chinese tradition. I fought hard to get here. I tell women who feel trapped by their circumstances that they need the courage and determination to bring change. My message, number one, is that a way out is possible. Number two, you have to take the first step. Number three, you have to start now because everyone is waiting around for someone else to start, so nothing happens. You can do it!"*

I felt as if she were speaking directly to me. The magic of her voice, the intensity of her caring was inviting. I was curious about Dhammananda's relationship to her mother, Venerable

---

*TEDxDoiSuthep—Dhammananda Bhikkhuni—Empowering Our Potentiality

Voramai. I had seen her mother's photograph hanging in the temple bookstore. What struck me initially was the family resemblance between mother and daughter, but their expressions were completely different. Dhammananda was often smiling in pictures, and her eyes radiated a soft light. In contrast, her mother looked intimidating with her dark brown eyes, shaved head, and stern expression. Questions lingered. How old had Dhammananda been when her mother was ordained? What was it like to grow up in a monastic setting? Why did Dhammananda decide to be ordained? Did her mother pressure her into the decision? I made a mental note to explore these questions when I interviewed her.

I began to get anxious about an hour into the lecture, anticipating our meeting. I knew I wanted to interview her, but what if she said no? At the break I made my way to the front of the room.

Dhammananda was looking down at the ground, deep in thought. I greeted her with the traditional *wai*, bowing in her presence and waiting for a sign of recognition. Dhammananda's eyes went blank. No special greeting, no heartfelt reunion. From her reaction, I realized that Dhammananda didn't remember me. A pang shot through my heart. In my fantasy I'd replayed the scene a thousand times; there was a joyous reunion and friendship. Instead, I sat before a contemplative woman fully immersed in the present moment. It dawned on me that many women visit the temple, and she couldn't possibly remember all those faces. Although I felt hurt, I was determined to pursue the relationship. I proposed my story idea.

"I would like to write an article about your life for *Sawaddi Magazine*," I said. Can I interview you?"

"Sure," Dhammananda said.

"Are you available the second week of June?"

"I travel a lot. My schedule is at the temple. Just email me and we'll set up a time."

Even though the reunion didn't turn out as I had imagined, she'd granted my request. I was happy to know that I would see her again so I could pursue a relationship with her. I needed something to look forward to, and writing the article gave me the sense of purpose and direction that I had been seeking all along. I contacted Dhammananda via email when I got home, and we arranged to meet.

My next visit to the temple was in mid-June, four months after my surgery and eight months after that first visit where I'd had such a powerful experience during alms round and discovered the Medicine Buddha. I was excited and happy for the first time in months. I touched my back, smiling. My pain was getting better, and I was on a steady path to full recovery. I had started Pilates two days a week and was taking less medication. I began to feel hopeful that the surgery had been the right decision after all. I felt like a butterfly emerging from its cocoon. I wanted to spread my wings and fly.

On the drive to the temple, I asked my driver to stop at a roadside stand to buy flowers for the nuns: purple-and-white orchids, white daisies with green centers, and yellow marigolds. I glanced over the questions I had prepared for the interview and set them aside for later. I wondered how Dhammananda would receive me. Would she be friendly? Would she be distant? We drove past the full-bellied Chinese Buddha and pulled into the front parking lot. As soon as we passed through the temple gates, time began moving in slow motion. My concerns of home dissipated. I liked the anonymity of coming to the temple where there were no expectations. I connected to a deeper sense of myself beyond my role as wife and mother. I knew Dhammananda had been married and had three sons before she left her family to become a nun. I wondered if she'd ever gone through a period of questioning her life's path.

Five barking dogs ran up to meet my car. One dog was wagging her tail. She looked like a cross between a Dalmatian and a dachshund, white with black spots but short and squat. I stooped down to pet her, and she rolled over to have her stomach rubbed. I learned later that she was called Dot Com. When I looked up, Dhammavanna was coming out of the office, walking toward me. She was the woman who greeted me when I first visited the temple. She smiled. "It's good to see you again. Are you staying overnight?"

"Not this time. I'm just here for the afternoon to meet with Dhammananda."

"I will let her know you are here. You can wait here in the office where it's cooler."

Once inside I browsed the books and CDs for sale. Before long I saw Dhammananda striding toward the office, strong and agile. She was so radiant. I felt a tinge of excitement as she approached.

Smiling, she waved at me. "Come, we will go to the cafeteria." As we headed outside, she opened an umbrella. "Here, take it, the sun is so strong today," she insisted. We walked over to the dining area, a wide-open rectangular space with a wooden roof, two rows of ceiling fans, and long metal tables with blue plastic chairs. Even though it was hot, the overhead fans generated a cool breeze that made the heat tolerable. Dhammananda made her way to a metal table.

"Come, sit here." She patted the seat next to her.

"I have a new art book to show you," she said. Flipping

through it, she pointed to a photograph of a mural painting in which two lines of women followed the Buddha in procession.

"These are the first women bhikkhunis ordained by the Buddha. They are the thirteen Arahat Theris." She smiled. "The women at the National Museum told me about the painting when I lectured there in May. I saw the picture two weeks ago at Wat Po, near the ceiling behind the Buddha's head."

I had seen Wat Po, the temple famous for its statue of the reclining Buddha lying on his right side.

"The museum volunteers bought the book for me. Now when people ask me, I can show them the picture," she said beaming. I had my list of questions but set them aside. I felt a deep yearning to connect with Dhammananda on a more personal level. I wanted to let her know all I had been through, so I confided to her that I'd had surgery. She expressed concern about how I was doing. We talked about my experiences, and eventually I mentioned my connection to the Medicine Buddha. "I've been chanting to the Medicine Buddha, and it's helping me heal."

"Good, good," she cooed. Now it was her turn to share. "Let me show you the drawings for the Medicine Buddha shrine. I drew them myself." She showed me a sketch of a building she called a *vihara* (monastery).

"The vihara will surround the Medicine Buddha. When it's built, we'll have a seven-day retreat to celebrate. Everyone will have to be vegetarian for a week, no meat."

"I would love to come for a week," I said.

"Sure, join us," she said. I was thrilled that she wanted to include me.

She leaned back in her chair and tilted her head to the side. "Let me tell you a story about the Medicine Buddha. It was 1994, when I was still a professor teaching Buddhist studies at Thammasat University." I tried to imagine

Dhammananda as a professor. I was curious to know what she looked like when she still had hair and dressed in conventional clothing, but couldn't quite picture it. I pulled my chair in closer to her. She was a marvelous storyteller, and I was riveted by her words.

"One day in meditation I saw an image of a healing Buddha sitting cross-legged. His kneecap had a flap-door where people could enter his body. He was seated in a beautiful valley with mountains around him. I couldn't understand what the vision meant." What struck me about her description was the dreamlike quality of the images, especially the flap-door—that really intrigued me. The image was so clear. I fantasized about Dhammananda entering the Buddha's body and traveling through his bloodstream on a giant raft. I felt childlike, full of wonder. My eyes opened wider to absorb more fully what she was saying.

In the three years following this vision, Dhammananda traveled to many countries searching for the Buddha image she had seen in her meditation. In Myanmar and Taiwan she asked healing masters if they could direct her to what she was looking for. She never found the Buddha she imagined, and didn't understand what her meditation meant until after she was ordained in 2001. She realized she was supposed to build her own sanctuary for the Medicine Buddha where sick people could come and chant. Then, as if to clarify her next point, she traced her finger on the table.

"I drew a sketch of the Medicine Buddha, like the one in my meditation, and gave it to a local sculptor. It took one year for him to create a finished wax model from my drawing. The Medicine Buddha you saw in the garden is 3.2 meters tall and the width at his knees is 2.7 meters. His body is made of brass, and his crown and forehead are made of gold. Lay members of the temple donated their gold earrings and chains to be melted down for the Buddha's head."

I marveled at people's generosity, parting with their jewelry as a sign of their devotion to Dhammananda and the Medicine Buddha. I also revered this Buddha, which surprised me since I had been raised Jewish. I thought about the admonition in the synagogue not to worship false idols. It wasn't just Judaism; the Buddha didn't encourage worshipping gods either. Yet here I was praying to this very real statue. I asked Dhammananda if my actions contradicted the Buddha's teachings.

"You could say that this image is nothing but a gimmick to draw people into the essence of the Buddha. But when you talk about the essence of the Buddha, people ask, who, where? People can't understand because it's too abstract. So if you can see something like this with your own eyes, you begin to feel the experience inside."

I understood what she was saying and responded eagerly. "I feel a real presence when I pray to the Medicine Buddha, like a spiritual companion. I have been reciting his healing chant ever since you gave me his picture on my first visit to the temple. I started before surgery, and now I pray to him every day."

Dhammananda acknowledged me with an emphatic, "Yes! Healing becomes possible when you have faith. But if you ask me is he real, if you start to question whether he will help you or not, you will not be healed. You must believe, and then healing can happen."

This made sense to me, and I nodded in agreement. I was living proof that prayer and faith were beneficial. I listened intently as Dhammananda continued to describe the healing powers of the Medicine Buddha.

"Tibetan Buddhists of antiquity believed that the Buddha's healing powers derived from a rare and precious gemstone, lapis lazuli, a natural dark blue stone found in the Himalayas. In Tibetan *thankgas* (religious paintings), the blue lapis color symbolizes the Buddha's healing radiance." Like a dry sponge, I was soaking in her words.

"Can I see the Medicine Buddha again?" I asked.

"No, he will be completely covered until the vihara is finished, so maybe another two years. We are still raising money for the building."

I was shocked and disappointed. I had no idea when I first saw the Buddha that he would only be uncovered that one day for a special ceremony. It never occurred to me that I would have to wait another two years to see him again. In hindsight, I wondered if my first encounter with the Medicine Buddha was providential. Was it idle curiosity that had drawn me into the garden that day, or was it the Medicine Buddha who, unannounced, escorted me there? Whatever the reason, I couldn't say, but for now I was going to have to wait to see him again. I figured that there was a lesson in this, something about understanding that I was not in control of the process, that I'd have to be patient and trust myself, and that all would be revealed in time.

Dhammananda looked pensive, deep in thought. In her moment of reflection, I felt her own healing radiance shine through. She had a softness about her that felt welcoming. Curious, I asked if she saw herself as a healer.

"Sometimes when I touch people, I invoke the grace of the Medicine Buddha for healing. I always pray really hard for them." She described three women with cancer whom she'd visited that same morning. "One woman in her last stage of cancer couldn't come outside during alms round. We went to her bedside. I held her in my arms while the nuns chanted the Buddha's blessing for her." Dhammananda lifted her hand to her heart. "It was very moving."

Adjusting her robes, Dhammananda said, "My mother was a great mystic and healer with a large following of supporters all over the country. Her ordained name was Venerable Voramai, but everyone affectionately called her Venerable Grandma. I am proud that Songdhammakalyani Temple carries on practices that my mother introduced more than fifty years ago." She paused in quiet reflection. The conversation had naturally come full circle—a perfect place to begin asking about her mother. I felt like the interview had begun in earnest, and I pulled out my questions to guide me.

"What was your relationship with your mother like?"

"She was the lawgiver. My mother had very high standards. She never gave me the impression that she was happy with me. I could never argue or discuss anything; I simply did what I was told."

I paused to consider what Dhammananda was saying. The way she described her mother as the "law giver" was so apropos of my own mother, who was strict and overbearing. I remember my mother asking me, "Did you do your chores like I asked? Make sure you do your homework before you go out to play." It was as if I were somehow deficient. She always had a string of tasks for me to complete. I even remember a little song I made up when I was five or six.

"I work so hard. I work all day and I never ever *ever* get a chance to play!"

Like Dhammananda, I was the "obedient" daughter. I never argued with my mother and simply did what I was told. Sadly, no matter how hard I tried, I never seemed to measure up to her expectations. She often found fault with me; why or what for, I never knew. I got used to her familiar refrain, "Go to your room and don't come out until you learn how to behave."

Being the good daughter, I always obeyed, but I was never exactly sure what I had done wrong. From an early age, I was consumed with shame and simply withdrew into myself, a simmering stew of hurt and resentment bubbling below the surface. When I was an adolescent, my mother and I had screaming matches, yelling at each other over mundane things. None of it made any sense, but we clung to each other in desperate hate like two fighters in a bear hug, unable to let go.

As an adult, I still heard my mother's critical voice rattling in my head. I fought hard to resist it, but her rejection stayed with me. I was a prisoner of my own negativity, a perspiring vessel of self-hatred. I didn't know how long I'd been lost in my own thoughts, but when I looked up, Dhammananda was sitting quietly petting the dog with the black and white spots, Dot Com. She was so caring and compassionate. A sudden realization came over me: *I am safe here. I can let go.* In that moment my heart softened. Tears welled up in me, and I began to cry.

Dhammananda reached out to touch me. "It's okay," she said. "People often cry when they first arrive. You build a wall around yourself, and that wall starts to crumble, and you allow that soft you to come out. I believe change comes from the heart, not from the intellect. You must feel it. If you have to weep, weep, and it opens you up and leads you to change." I felt as if she could see straight through to my soul.

"Your mother sounds so similar to my mother," I said. "Tell me more about her."

She told me how her mother had been a very capable journalist and writer, as well as an accomplished jujitsu practitioner and sword fencer. In the summer of 1932, she'd ridden on a bicycle with the Boy Scouts of Thailand from Bangkok to Singapore. It had taken her twenty-nine days.

Dhammananda told me the story of her mother's ordination, how it happened when she was ten years old on May 2, 1956. Her mother was tired of waiting for the monks to give her permission to be ordained, so she took Dhammananda, her only biological child, and her three adopted children to the barbershop, but didn't say anything. The kids stood against a back wall and watched while the barber cut off their mother's hair and shaved her head. It was so strange, Dhammananda said, but none of them spoke a word. This was typical of her mother, she explained, not to communicate with her children. After that, the family went to Wat Bovornnives where her mother received novice ordination from Pra Prommuni, her teacher and the deputy abbot of the temple.

Dhammananda remembered her mother saying to her, "My duty as a mother does not stop with my ordination." This had a profound impact on Dhammananda because Thai men leave their families when they receive ordination. Dhammananda didn't lose her mother because of her choice to become an ordained nun. She said that her mother's life was not easy because she was a single parent who supported the family on her own. Although never divorced, her mother had separated from her husband when Dhammananda was just three and a half.

Dhammananda came to a natural pause in her story. I wondered out loud, "If Thailand doesn't permit ordination, how was your mother treated?"

"Her path as a monastic was very lonely," she said pensively. Dhammananda explained that the Sangha officials challenged her mother about her ordained status, but her teacher had defended her, and that was the last time anyone registered an official complaint about her.

She paused to collect her thoughts. Then she recounted the story of how her mother had purchased a field of rice paddies near Nakon Pathom in 1960. Eventually she converted the land into temple grounds with a main prayer hall, meditation center, dining hall, living quarters, and an orphanage and school for eighty children. Dhammananda said she was proud that her mother was the first Thai woman to be ordained in the Mahayana tradition and that her mother spent forty-seven years in yellow robes.

Just then a nun in brown robes, Dhammatira, approached with an adorable little Thai girl with curly black hair who appeared to be about four. I looked down at my watch and realized we had been talking for about an hour. The child snuggled up to Dhammananda.

"This is my granddaughter, Naboon." She took her hand and hugged her. Dhammatira knelt before her as they spoke in Thai. Dhammananda excused herself, saying, "I have so many responsibilities here."

I thanked her for the interview and asked if I could come again soon. I had so many unanswered questions about her life. I'd learned about her mother, but I wanted to understand more of her personal journey and how she came to be ordained. For now, my questions would have to wait.

On the ride home, I felt exhilarated and inspired. I realized that the time we spent together had exceeded my expectations. What I thought was going to be a simple interview turned out to be a rich exchange with a wise healer. The slightest tilt of her head and the deep presence that radiated from her eyes told me she would reveal truths about me I never knew existed. It was the beginning of an intimate relationship with my beloved teacher who would provide the spiritual counsel I was seeking, and who would change my life forever.

*Dhammananda and I in the dining area of
the temple. June 2006*

Chapter 6:

Precious Gifts

Back home the ground underneath me was shifting. I was like a tiny leaf suspended from a branch, fluttering in the wind, hanging on by one thin thread to a former self who turned more and more to the temple as my spiritual anchor and home. Durga, now proficient in her domestic duties, ran the household with little direction from me except to help with meal planning. Since Randall worked during the week and rode his bicycle on the weekends, we spent less time together. Kris required less attention from me as he settled into his school routine. Now that my family didn't depend on me as much, I watched my identity as wife and mother float away like a white slip of paper, blowing in the wind. I worried that no one needed me and wrestled with feelings of insecurity.

Four months had passed since my surgery and my back felt stronger. I no longer had to concentrate on my recovery and had big blocks of free time, which terrified me. I wasn't sure why having so much free time scared me, but ever since childhood, my fear of the unknown had haunted me. Even as an adult, this fear still plagued me.

I woke up anxious most mornings, unsure of who I was or where I was headed. It reminded me of a similar dilemma I had faced those first few months in Thailand—what to do with the endless days that stretched before me.

The day after I returned from the temple, Monday morning, I woke before Randall, got dressed, and walked downstairs to a house filled with silence. Soon I heard Randall shuffling upstairs and put on the coffee pot. Randall soon joined me in the kitchen, and we talked about our plans for the day as he poured coffee into his commuter mug. He slung his computer bag over his shoulder and left for work with our driver as I opened the back patio screen doors to let in the cool, fresh morning air.

It was seven o'clock, my quiet time to pray to the Medicine Buddha before Kris and Durga got up. I sat in front of the picture of the Medicine Buddha perched on a Chinese step chest in our living room and recited the verses to his prayer to calm my mind. I had been chanting to the Medicine Buddha ever since my first visit to the temple eight months earlier, and now it felt like the most important ritual of my day. After reciting the prayer, I closed my eyes and meditated for twenty minutes. When I first sat down, my thoughts ran wild, hogging my attention, stretching my mind in awkward directions. *Don't forget to wake Kris soon. Make sure to water the plants in the bedroom. I should take the paintings we bought last weekend and have them framed today. I don't want to run out of coffee; make sure that's on Durga's shopping list. What is wrong with me? Why can't I just relax and clear my mind? I'm terrible at meditation. I don't know why I even try.*

Then I would come back to my breathing like Dhammananda had taught me. "Focus your attention on your nostrils," she would say. "Feel the stream of air as you inhale. Imagine blue healing light entering inside you, then let it go as you exhale." As I practiced, I got better at turning off my thoughts, if only for a few seconds at a time. I relished these moments of solitary time as a training opportunity to quiet the endless chatter of my mind. Meditating helped me face the day with less anxiety.

I woke Kris up about seven thirty for summer school. Half an hour later, he trudged downstairs with his backpack over his shoulder. He didn't say much, just grabbed a granola bar and headed out the door. Now in ninth grade, he drove a golf cart to school, picking up his buddies along the way. All the boys his age could be seen puttering down the streets of Nichada, weaving and laughing as they roamed the neighborhoods of the compound in their golf carts. My responsibilities for Kris were pretty simple. I oversaw his schoolwork, occasionally hiring tutors for him or attending teacher conferences. Many afternoons, Durga made him chocolate chip cookies as a treat. On weekends Kris headed into Bangkok with his friends. Already proficient in Thai, he communicated easily with the taxi drivers who took him downtown. Kris' newly acquired independence left me free to explore new opportunities.

After Kris left, I sat down at the kitchen counter to peruse recipes. I always chose the daily menu so Durga would know what to cook and what ingredients to buy. Glancing through the cookbooks, I found a fried chicken recipe that Kris liked. Some nights when I didn't have any suggestions for dinner, Durga cooked elaborate meals—Burmese curry dishes, sautéed greens, and fresh Indian bread called roti, accompanied by trays of fresh sliced fruit. Randall, Kris, and I adored her cooking.

I stared at my lukewarm coffee. My life at home felt like a photograph in shades of black and white. I felt my familiar nemesis, depression, creeping up on me again. I didn't want to fall into the familiar black hole. I asked myself, *What do I really want to do?* My thoughts drifted to the temple. I loved chanting in the early mornings with the women. Joining in unison with their shimmering voices felt like being embraced in a sacred circle of song. I cocked my head and listened intently as if the women were singing with me now. Still suspended in thought, I heard the kitchen door open behind me.

Durga shuffled in carrying the laundry basket filled with clean clothes perched on her hip. Sitting atop the stack of laundry was Durga's constant companion, Ringo, a special cat we'd purchased last Christmas at the weekend market. She was called a Scottish fold because her ears flopped over rather than standing erect. Ringo, so named by Kris in honor of Ringo Starr, was supposed to be his cat, but she had bonded with Durga, trailing behind her and batting her bare feet as she walked through the house.

"Morning, madam."

"Good morning, Durga. Were you up late doing laundry?"

"Yes, madam. I finish ironing Randall shirts."

"What time did you go to bed?" I asked.

"Maybe midnight, not sure. How was the temple?"

"It was fantastic. I love the temple women and spending time with Dhammananda."

"Oh, madam, you look so happy when you come back from the temple." Durga set her basket down, and Ringo scampered out of it.

"What you do there?" Durga asked.

"We chant in the morning and then go on alms round. In the evening, we pray again. After evening chanting, Dhammananda invites all the women to sit in a circle on the floor and talk about what happened to them that day." Ringo slid up to Durga, content to rub against her calf. I knew that

Durga sometimes prayed at a nearby temple on Buddhist holidays and asked her if she had gone recently.

"I go next week for special celebration. I pray for you and sir and Kris. Want you to be happy." Durga's kindness touched me. She had so little compared to us, a migrant with no papers or status as far as the Thais were concerned, yet she never bore resentment toward us or complained; she had an inner strength all her own. When we needed her, she was there. Even though she called me *madam*, I felt like her student following her wise example of how to live a compassionate life. I didn't realize it then, but years later I would understand that Durga became the emotional fulcrum of our family during our time in Thailand. Grateful for the help, I never felt threatened or jealous that she had replaced me as caretaker.

"Thank you, Durga. Maybe you can come and visit the temple with me sometime. I think you would like it."

Durga smiled and noticed the list on the counter. "What you want me to cook tonight, madam?"

I handed her the shopping list, and she headed upstairs to deliver the laundry, Ringo trailing behind her. My thoughts drifted back to the temple. I liked the anonymity of going, shedding the persona of wife and mother to explore a deeper part of myself.

I started concocting a plan to go back, even though I'd just been there. I wondered how soon I could return and whether Nancy would like to go with me. She was an excellent photographer and might be willing to take pictures for my article. I reached for the phone to call her. She loved the idea of going, but suggested we stay for one night instead of two. Though I would have preferred to stay longer, I agreed, and we made a plan to head down on a Saturday afternoon and return Sunday evening the first weekend in July, just two weeks away.

On Sundays the nuns collected alms, and I wanted Nancy to have that experience. I called the main office number at the temple to see if there was room. Usually Dhammavanna picked up.

"Hallo," a sweet voice answered.

"Dhammavanna?" I asked.

"Yes. Who's this?"

"Cindy."

"Sandy!" Dhammavanna mispronounced my name, but I took it as a sign of endearment that she now recognized me. "You come to the temple?" She sounded excited.

"Can I bring a friend?" We spoke briefly, and she assured me the bungalow would be available. I thought about contacting Dhammananda to meet with her, but decided to wait. I had just seen her and didn't want to appear too needy, though to be honest I craved her attention. Shame shot through me like a hot arrow piercing my chest. *Restrain yourself*, my critical mother voice echoed in my head. I pulled back the reins of my inner desires and decided to wait and see what happened. Spontaneity was a foreign word in my vocabulary, but just this once, I would let the story unfold on its own terms. I sighed and stared out the window. The two-week wait to return to the temple stretched before me like an eternity.

I felt adrift, like a stranger in my own skin. It wasn't an unfamiliar feeling to me, but nevertheless it took me by surprise. If you've ever passed yourself in the mirror and done a double take at the person staring back at you, you know this experience. I knew it was a combination of things bringing it on, but primarily an old version of myself was dying, and I didn't know who I was.

Now that Durga was taking care of us, Kris and Randall no longer needed me in the same way. Whatever person I expected myself to be, whatever role I had played in the family suddenly vanished. Change brings about a profound sense of loss and a longing for parts of our self that have gone missing. We search frantically for our identity in the face of uncertainty. Perhaps that's why we embark on the spiritual journey—to uncover who we are in the process of becoming.

When Saturday morning came, I packed up a few essentials— toothpaste, toothbrush, and one indulgence, my pillow. I dressed in white just like the maejis, as a sign of respect. I wondered how Nancy, a lefty liberal from New York who questioned authority of any kind, would react to Dhammananda. I wanted her to revere my teacher, to experience the rapture of sitting in meditation with the women, to be inspired like me. It was probably foolish of me to expect so much from a self-professed nonbeliever, but I couldn't help myself.

It was mid-afternoon when we drove past the Chinese Buddha, through the gates, and into the temple. The dogs barked, announcing our arrival. Although slightly menacing, the dogs made a lot of noise initially but soon calmed down. Not reacting was the best ploy. Nancy and I stepped out of the car and wove our way through the racket to the main office. Dhammavanna was sitting inside working on her laptop. She looked up and smiled.

"Hello, Sandy." She stood up, adjusting her robe.

I bowed before Dhammavanna and turned to introduce my companion.

"This is my friend Nancy."

"Ahh, you come back to the temple to see Venerable Mother?" she asked.

My heart leaped at that possibility. I wouldn't turn down the opportunity if offered. "Is she available?"

"I check," Dhammavanna said. Taking a key from the desk drawer, she led us down the main path to the same bungalow I'd stayed in with Marilyn that first visit.

"We gather in the garden at four o'clock. You join us." Dhammavanna turned to close the front door behind her. I noticed a picture of the Dalai Lama hung there, and wondered if Dhammananda knew the Dalai Lama. If so, how had they met and what was their relationship like? I made a mental note to ask her about that if we had a chance to talk.

In the room I saw a plaque on the wall that I hadn't seen before. It described the history of the bungalow named Baan Rom Ruen. Rom was Dhammananda's paternal great-grandmother's name and Ruen was her eldest son. Dhammananda had occupied this room from 1983 to 1999 and written many of her published books there. After her ordination, she'd renamed it the *Dhamma* (Buddhist teaching) guesthouse and dedicated it to her ancestors. I liked the idea of staying in the room where Dhammananda had written all her books. I'd always held a secret aspiration to be a writer and wondered if this might be an invitation for me to get started.

I motioned to Nancy and said, "Let's go explore." Nancy took her camera out of its case and slung it around her neck. We walked out into the blazing afternoon sun and down the central path where Dhammavanna was walking toward us.

"Venerable Mother can see you now. You go to her office by the cafeteria."

As we walked toward the office, dark clouds gathered announcing imminent showers. I felt nervous, afraid that Nancy would do something odd in the presence of my spiritual teacher. *Does she even believe in God?* I wondered. Now was not the best time to be raising this question, but it did cross my mind. Always the good girl, I didn't want Nancy to challenge or question Dhammananda. I silently pleaded, *Don't say anything to embarrass me, don't question authority, just sit quietly and revere her like I do. Just be respectful, please.*

Dhammananda looked up as we approached.

"Come," she motioned to us, her radiant smile welcoming us. "I see you brought a friend. I love it when you bring your friends!" I bowed in respect. Nancy stood blithely at my side as if unfazed by all that was happening around her. Raindrops fell in gentle pings on the tin roof overhead. The air cooled slightly. We pulled up two chairs.

I hadn't come prepared with questions but recalled seeing the Dalai Lama's photograph and asked Dhammananda about it. "There is a beautiful picture of His Holiness in our room."

"Oh yes." She smiled. "The first time I met His Holiness was 1980. I was sitting in the waiting room outside his office and could hear him giggling and laughing with someone else. His laughter was so contagious I couldn't help but laugh along with him. We talked for some time, and when I left the whole world looked so different. I was overjoyed. When I visit His Holiness, I take it as an initiation to a new life, a new understanding." I felt the same way after spending time with Dhammananda—more alive and aware of my surroundings.

Dhammananda fell easily into the conversational style we'd been cultivating over our visits. She expanded her answers for me as always, no doubt noticing that I drank in everything she said. I felt as if I were in a bubble, just she and

I. My control and concern over Nancy's behavior evaporated. If Nancy had walked out while Dhammananda was talking, I surely wouldn't have noticed. Dhammananda explained how she had never asked the Dalai Lama to be her guru but nevertheless felt he was. Once, she said, he was leading chanting with thousands of people, and when he saw her take her seat in the front row, he waved.

Nancy pulled my attention away for a moment as she shifted in her seat, looking uncomfortable. I explained to Dhammananda that it was thanks to Nancy that I'd heard about her lecture in May at the National Museum. Dhammananda noticed the camera around Nancy's neck.

"My father gave me my first camera when I was twelve," she said. "He really liberated me from the traditional female stereotypes by encouraging me to do whatever I wanted. He never let me get away with the excuse that I couldn't do it because I was a girl. He broke all the rules. Wherever I travel, I take my camera with me." She leaned forward slightly. "Will you take pictures tomorrow morning during alms round?"

Nancy's face lit up. "I'd be happy to."

"Let me show you something." Dhammananda pointed to the white curtains behind her. She drew them open, revealing a painting of a beautiful seated woman with long ears, gold earrings, a gold necklace, and a gold headpiece. "This is Tara, the Tibetan embodiment of wisdom." Robes of deep orange and light blue draped her arms, and her right breast was exposed. Her right palm was open, and in her left hand she held the stem of a huge pink peony. "Just as his Holiness the Dalai Lama is the Bodhisattva of Compassion, I draw spiritual energy from Tara, the Bodhisattva of Wisdom." It struck me how influenced Dhammananda had been by Tibetan Buddhism, and I asked her if that conflicted with her Theravada beliefs.

"I draw from other Buddhist traditions, too," she explained. She told us how, when she made the decision to be ordained, it was hard for her to choose between Theravada and Tibetan Buddhism because of her close connection to the Dalai Lama. Also, she found Tibetan texts more meaningful than the Theravada, even though, eventually, she took ordination in the Theravada tradition. I found it fascinating that she honored other traditions. I felt a kindred spirit in her. Even though I had been raised Jewish, I was inspired by Buddhist rituals and teachings, and since arriving in Thailand, I was much more involved with meditation and prayer than I had ever been with the Jewish religion. Our family celebrated Jewish holidays and went to synagogue until I was twelve, but I hadn't returned since then. As a child, I loved the special foods and rituals associated with Passover, Rosh Hashanah, and Yom Kippur, but the holiday I loved most was the spring celebration of Purim.

When I was five, my mother drove my sister and me to Sunday school. I had a powerful imagination and loved the Purim story that honors Queen Esther, the bravest and most beautiful woman in all of Jewish history. The Persian King Ahasuerus chose Esther as his queen, and she saved the Jews from their Persian enemies. She was my heroine, and I imagined her adorned in robes of purple silk and blue satin with bracelets that jangled as she walked arm in arm with the king in courtly procession.

One Sunday our teacher, Mrs. Silver, announced that the following week we would have a contest. Each child would choose their favorite Purim character and come dressed in costume. Parents and family members would be sitting in the audience. Whoever got the loudest applause would win a prize. Mrs. Silver gave us art supplies to create the ideal crown or hat to go with our costume. I determined that my queen must have a crown. I cut pointed edges on a piece of cardboard, covered it in aluminum foil, dabbed glue on the surface, and sprinkled gold, silver, and red sequins on it. I sat back and admired my creation.

"Beautiful," the teacher said as she laid it on a shelf to dry.

The next week came, and my mom must have forgotten about the contest. When I saw all the other kids, excited and running around in costume, my heart sank. There were several Hamans (the bad guy) with their three-cornered hats, two Uncle Mordecais (Esther's uncle), and three girls dressed as Queen Esther. I wanted to be Queen Esther in the worst way. Devastated, I started to cry. Mrs. Silver walked over and put her hands on my shoulders. She took my hand, led me into a back room, and pointed out three cardboard boxes filled with leftover costumes. There, she pulled out a big, blue denim box-shaped top and a floor-length, plain matching skirt. I looked at the sacks and thought, *No way Queen Esther would wear that.*

"You want me to wear that? I asked the teacher.

"Yes."

"But Queen Esther wouldn't wear that." I was only five, but I knew something was amiss. I had a sinking feeling in my stomach as I pulled the top over my shirt and the skirt over my shorts, looking like a big blue sack of potatoes. *I'll win the booby prize for sure.* Fortunately, I had my crown and a string of white pop beads in my pocket that I strung around my neck.

All the children lined up and we walked over to the auditorium and climbed the stairs leading to the stage. We waited behind the wings as the audience arrived. Mrs. Silver called us out one by one. When she called my name, my cheeks reddened with embarrassment. *How can I go out looking like this?*

"Now, Queen Esther," Mrs. Silver announced as I walked onto center stage with my head down. Then the strangest thing happened: people hooted and clapped. They liked me. When I reached the other side of the stage, I had a big smile on my face.

After the contest, the teacher brought us back on stage. A woman's voice called out, "Queen Esther, first prize." *Which one?* I wondered. *There are four Queen Esthers.*

The rabbi motioned in my direction. *Did he mean me?* I couldn't believe it. The rabbi walked toward me and handed me a blue ribbon. Overjoyed with my prize, a new feeling of confidence filled me. Looking back as an adult, I've since characterized this as an "Aha!" moment, when I received praise and acknowledgment simply for being myself. It's a precious memory from childhood when I was validated—a singular moment that, sadly, happened all too infrequently when I was growing up. As an adult, I have to consciously work at accepting myself. On occasion, when I can recall the experience, I bolster my self-confidence with this simple reminder and whisper to myself, *Remember Queen Esther.*

I gazed up, scanning the painting as Dhammananda continued speaking. "My artistic son is painting it for me," Dhammananda said. "It's not quite finished."

This was the first time I'd heard her mention her son. Curious, I asked how her sons felt about her being ordained.

"My second son asked me directly, 'Did Venerable Grandma force you to do this?' "

"No, I told him, it is my choice." Dhammananda shifted forward in her seat. "All three of my sons accepted my decision, but my eldest son had a difficult time letting go at first. He said, 'I had to sacrifice my mother to the Buddha. I can't hug or touch her anymore.' "

I noticed Nancy lean forward in her chair, and turned to catch a confused look on her face, which Dhammananda surely caught, too, because she elaborated, "Thai bhikkhunis are not supposed to come into contact with a member of the opposite sex, so bhikkhunis cannot touch a man or a boy." She looked down at her hands with a pensive expression. She said she worried about her eldest son because he was going through a difficult separation from his wife. "You can listen and have compassion when people suffer, but it's hard when it's your own son. I had to deepen my practice and find an emotional anchor within myself."

Just then Nancy stood up and announced unceremoniously, "I'm going to take some pictures." I was embarrassed and a little angry. How could she be so rude as to make this announcement just as Dhammananda had shared something so personal and intimate? But Dhammananda was unfazed. I marveled at her ability to stay present and remain calm when I was feeling anything but.

Speaking in a quiet voice, she asked, "You remember that woman I told you about on alms round? The one with cancer?"

"Yes."

"She died two days ago. Now she no longer suffers." She held her hand to her heart. "Her daughter told me she asked for me, but I was in Bangkok, so she recited the Medicine Buddha chant to her mother as she died." Dhammananda continued to speak in low tones, confiding in me. She said that the woman's physical suffering at the end of her life burned up her negative kharma so she could now be born again, renewed. I felt drawn into Dhammananda's personal world, like a special guest invited into an inner sanctum. I appreciated her sharing her innermost thoughts and wondered if she ever felt lonely, or if she had people in her life she confided in about personal matters. I relied on her personal guidance, but whom could she talk to? I asked her, fishing a bit, "Do you ever feel lonely?"

Dhammananda's face grew stern. "Walking the bodhisattva's path, we do not have time for loneliness. We receive all the good energy, and I rely on my faith in the Buddha to support me." I felt embarrassed that somehow I had crossed a sacred boundary, and she had reprimanded me. Still, part of me wondered, I seemed to have touched a nerve—maybe she actually did suffer at times, but didn't want to admit it.

I changed the topic. "What is hard about ordained life?"

Dhammananda laughed. "Getting up at five o'clock. I never wanted to get up that early. And I miss eating blueberry cheesecake. I used to love high tea in the afternoon. I would like to have a Sunday off, but you cannot have your Sunday off. This living in community, you really have to let go of yourself. There is no such thing as personal time. Like when the bell rings at seven o'clock for breakfast. I wish I could finish writing this article, but no, I have to put down my work, respect others."

I had seen Dhammananda at mealtimes. Everyone waited for her to enter the room and take her seat at her private table before starting. Once she sat down, the nuns served themselves food and gave a blessing. Then the maejis' turn came, along with any laywomen or temple visitors. She said, "The respect that you ask from others is the same respect and responsibility you must offer them." I wondered, since my family role as primary caretaker had shifted, how I could fulfill my commitments to my husband and son. Before I could seek advice from Dhammananda, though, the gong rang, signaling that it was time to work in the garden.

"Come with me," she said. "We will do Chi Gung."

Everyone gathered in the garden. The late afternoon light was a golden tone. I looked around for Nancy, but she was nowhere to be seen. Dhammananda took her place in front of the women, her arms gently resting at her side. She signaled to me. "Cindy, come stand opposite me so you can follow what I'm doing." When Dhammananda singled me out from the rest of the group, a secret feeling of satisfaction filled me. The needy part of me wanted her to like me best. Like a starving animal, I lapped up her attention. Unable to acknowledge myself, I looked to her for validation. I figured if someone as important as Dhammananda cared that much about me, I must be worthy after all.

Dhammananda led us through a series of fifteen exercises. I watched her hands, so poised and graceful, like soft petals floating to the ground. As I followed her movements, I felt the grass underneath my bare feet and a solid connection to the earth. As we finished the Chi Gung, Nancy joined us in the garden. I was no longer as upset with her. Maybe it was the Chi Gung, but I felt calmer and wanted to be more tolerant of her.

Dhammavanna and I sat down in the grass side by side. As Nancy approached, I invited her to sit with us. "Thanks, but I think I would rather take pictures," she said. She pulled her camera eye level, focused her lens on Dhammavanna and me, and clicked the shutter. She approached Dhammananda and asked if she could take her picture. Dhammananda nodded. Once again, I was embarrassed and worried that Nancy was intruding on her.

As Dhammavanna and I sat together, we pulled slender weeds out of the grass. She talked to me about seventy deaf students who had recently visited the temple. Dhammavanna said when the nuns chanted, the teachers signed and the children sang along. Her eyes opened wide as she described this. "It was so beautiful, it touched my heart."

Dhammavanna and I were becoming closer. She seemed to like me, and the feeling was mutual. I trusted her and confided in her that I felt disconnected at home, not sure how to care for my husband and son.

Dhammavanna told me, "You have to love yourself before you can love someone else. It begins here, in your heart." She tenderly touched her hand to her chest. "You must care for yourself in order to care for others." Dhammavanna's words landed gently on my ears. Soothed by her advice, I returned to the task at hand, plucking weeds from the grass. It was slow work but gave me time to think. All my life I treated myself like a bad weed rather than a precious flower—the wounded child, unworthy and unlovable. I would pick away at my insecurities like a scab, unable to acknowledge my strengths. No wonder I looked to Dhammananda for praise. I thought about my sincere desire to become strong within myself. Granted, I needed practice and guidance from others, but eventually I hoped to learn to stand on my own two feet and walk with confidence. *I can do this. I have many spiritual teachers, Durga, Dhammavanna, and Dhammananda, all supporting me along my journey.* A calm assurance filled me that I would arrive at my destination if I continued to walk the path of my healing journey.

As afternoon transitioned into evening, Nancy and I headed to the eating area for dinner. Afterwards we joined the others for evening chanting and meditation. Seated in silent meditation, I heard shuffling. Opening my eyes slightly, I saw Nancy stand up and wander out. My stomach tightened. I wanted to yell, *What the hell?* But Dhammananda always said we poison ourselves with our anger, so I admonished myself even as the anger continued to rise up inside me. *Why are you upset? Stop taking it personally. Let go and let her be. This is not about you.* Partly selfish on my part, I didn't want Nancy's disrespectful behavior to reflect back on me. I felt like a little girl in a tantrum. I wanted Nancy to be spiritual like me so I could feel good about myself. Instead, she had the audacity to be her own person with separate needs and desires. I wandered back to our room, irritated and grumbling to myself, *Why did I bring her in the first place?*

Later that night I questioned myself. What fueled my anger? A wise person once told me that anger can be a cover for shame. My shame stemmed from the deeply held belief that something was wrong with me. I always looked to others for validation when, in reality, I didn't know how to love myself. If I stepped back and looked at the situation dispassionately, I had to admit that Nancy's strength of character impressed me. Tired of meditating, she got up and left. While I ran around placating everyone, she moved to the rhythm of her own beat. Maybe Nancy had something to teach me. Finally, in a moment of clarity, I realized that Nancy wasn't there to accommodate my needs; whatever she did or did not do had nothing to do with my self-worth. I breathed a sigh of relief, finally able to let go.

The rest of our time spent at the temple passed quickly. During the early morning alms round the next day, I watched Nancy dart in and out of the procession taking photographs. Not wanting to be distracted, I concentrated on my breathing. *One step inhale, one step exhale.* With each step I imagined roots growing out the soles of my feet, connecting to the earth, grounding me in my experience. The remainder of our time at the temple, I continued to focus on myself. Throughout breakfast I remained silent, even though Nancy and I sat together. After breakfast, I chanted and meditated with the other women. I even lost track of Nancy until it was time to leave at midday. I found her seated near the front office, waiting with her overnight bag. As we watched for our driver, I asked Nancy to pull out her camera so I could look at the photos. It was a collage of our experiences—beautiful shots of Dhammananda accepting flowers from devotees on alms round, a child putting an offering of rice into Dhammanan-da's bowl, a picture of the smiling Chinese Buddha at the temple entrance, and a portrait of Venerable Voramai as a young woman taken from a black and white photo hanging in the office.

"These are incredible! They'll be perfect for my article."

"Thanks."

As I flipped through the images, one in particular took my breath away—a head shot of Dhammananda with a radiant smile and a look of utter delight on her face.

"When did you take this?" I asked.

Nancy paused and leaned in to inspect the shot. "Yesterday afternoon when you were working in the garden."

I couldn't help but smile; the irony of that moment did not escape me. At the time, I'd worried that Nancy had intruded on Dhammananda's space. Clearly I'd been mistaken. Dhammananda had practically glowed with excitement at having her picture taken. On the ride home I gushed over the photos and thanked Nancy for accompanying me.

Years later, I would come to realize that the picture Nancy took of Dhammananda that day in the garden was one of the most beautiful photographs of Dhammananda I had ever seen. For years it has graced the walls of my bedroom. Looking back on that experience with Nancy, I learned several things. It is important to let go of our expectations of others, of who we think they should be. When we stop focusing on ourselves and come to accept others as they truly are, we receive precious gifts that we never imagined possible.

Portrait of Dhammananda, which hangs in my bedroom.
Taken by Nancy Zarider, June 2006

Chapter 7:

A Place Called Home

Back home, family life grew more complicated as I continued to feel unanchored. My connection to my husband was no longer as defined as it had been in the first ten years of our marriage. In those early years, we enjoyed taking strenuous bike rides through the Berkeley Hills. We invested in a Ranger twenty-three-foot sailboat and sailed on San Francisco Bay on the weekends. Under heavy winds, I would take the tiller to steer the boat while Randall jumped onto the foredeck to change the sail. Confident in the driver's seat, I had full control of the boat. Our partnership was finely tuned, like a dance where we anticipated one another's moves. He was the captain; I was his first mate. I would haul in the sail at just the right moment when he yelled, "Hard alee," and the sail would blow over to the other side. Occasionally we would sail out to Angel Island and anchor for the night. The peaceful bobbing of the boat lulled us to sleep. We woke early and heated water for coffee on the camping stove. Mornings were serene; this was a blissful time in our lives.

Now I looked back on our early years of marriage from a different perspective. The heavier the wind, the greater the challenge, the more elated Randall felt, while I retreated inside. Randall thrived on being on the edge. Still in my mid-thirties, I wanted to prove to Randall that I could keep up. We took long bicycle rides with him in the lead. I pushed myself hard to impress him, even though I really wanted to slow down and ride at a more relaxed pace. Sometimes, I felt lonely but would never admit it to myself.

On one ride we crested a steep hill, me trailing behind Randall. My legs burned with the strain of the uphill climb as Randall pulled out of sight. It was a hot day, and I had my period. Sweat poured down my face. Nauseated, I could barely keep myself from throwing up. I was seething with anger and defiantly got off my bike and walked the steepest part. Randall would never consider doing such a thing. *I hate this,* I thought. *Who am I trying to impress?* I sacrificed my needs to accommodate my husband, but all I ever felt was second best. Even so, I didn't voice any of my discontent at that time. It would take years for me to recognize that Randall and I simply had different needs, and that I had to speak up for myself.

At age forty-five, I took my last bike ride with Randall and Kris. We were in Lake Tahoe, and we rode that day under a beautiful blue sky. The lake sparkled in the sunlight as we circled its perimeter. After the ride, I noticed my back was stiff but didn't pay much attention. Two weeks later, I experienced excruciating pain down my left leg when a disc ruptured in my lower back. Unbeknownst to me then, this was the beginning of a chronic lower back problem that would plague me for the next nine years. I sought help though a combination of medical interventions, including cortisone shots, a nerve block, physical therapy, and one unsuccessful attempt at back surgery.

In those first few years, Randall accompanied me to doctor's appointments, took time off work when I had surgery, and encouraged me whenever I felt disheartened. However, the injury eventually took a toll on our relationship. Of necessity, we spent less time together and more time apart. While I slowed down to pursue a path of physical healing, Randall continued his outdoor activities and adventure.

It wasn't intentional on the part of either of us, but by the time we moved to Bangkok, eight years after that initial injury, the fabric of our marriage had begun to fray. Randall had become less supportive over time. When I chose to pursue disc replacement surgery in Munich, he was initially skeptical that anything more could be done to improve my situation. Perhaps that's why he didn't accompany me to Germany. I have no way of knowing what he felt; I just sensed a growing distance between us. We still traveled together, taking exotic family vacations to Japan, Hong Kong, Singapore, and Vietnam, and we enjoyed ourselves. But I was moving along a spiritual path, unaccompanied by my husband. An agnostic, Randall wasn't drawn to spirituality like I was. While he enjoyed outdoor adventure, I preferred quiet contemplation and stillness. He remained constantly active, whereas I relished my quiet time. Like a flower bending toward the light, I turned to the temple for spiritual guidance. It became my refuge, and I began to spend more time there.

Dhammananda and I met again in mid-October to celebrate after the temple's annual three-month Rains Retreat, commonly referred to in Thai as *Vassa* or Buddhist Lent. This tradition dates back to the early days of Buddhism when nuns and monks typically sought shelter from the heavy rains, and did not travel far from the monastery. I had come for the *Kathina*, the official robes ceremony on a Sunday, almost a year to the day of my first visit to the temple. Visiting the monastery was like pausing the hands of a clock. All sense of time evaporated as I left my calendar behind. No longer bound by a schedule or responsibilities to others, I began to explore my authentic self—beyond the prescribed roles of wife and mother. I felt like a deep-sea diver, swimming below the surface in search of pearls of wisdom that lay buried in my depths.

Crowds of people ambled about—men, women, elders, teens, and young children. The hot mid-morning sun was strong. On this special occasion, the nuns had tied bright blue and yellow silk banners along the fences. A voice came over the loudspeaker in Thai, and people formed a line. In front, seated in a wheelchair, was an elderly woman half-hidden behind an elaborate flower arrangement balanced on her lap. A young man walked at her side holding a huge umbrella overhead. Behind him, a woman carried what looked like a small bush, but upon closer inspection I saw it was individual bills rolled up to look like flowers on a money tree of sorts. Young women followed, dressed in brightly colored, floor-length skirts that wrapped around their waists. I joined the end of the procession. Firecrackers popped in the background, and Thai music blared from the loudspeakers.

The parade wound its way slowly from the dining area to the main prayer hall and up three flights of steep stairs. The space on the third floor was a large, rectangular room about three times as large as the second-floor prayer hall where we did morning and evening chanting. There must have been at least two hundred people kneeling on floor mats, and another row of people seated in chairs in the back where I joined them. The air was stuffy. Ceiling fans hummed, and warm air blew through the crowd. Soon the people started chanting. I loved being swept up in the magic of their song. There was something mysterious and beautiful about the chanting. Similar to when I was a child, I felt drawn into the ritual— the voices, the smell of burning incense, the glittering Buddhas. The whole experience opened my senses to the divine. Dhammananda sat in a chair up front with a microphone. To her right was a table laden with food that must have been collected during morning alms round, and behind her were three rows of golden Buddha statues. A woman knelt before her and chanted a mournful tune. Rocking slightly, Dhammananda closed her eyes. When the woman stopped singing, Dhammananda began a Dhamma talk, first speaking in Thai and then translating into English. Her talk centered around the mind and the body. She spoke about the wisdom of the body. "The mind goes nonstop. If the mind dwells on something really heavy," she explained, "the body cannot carry it. Something that hurt us five years ago, the mind still dwells on it. It is the mind that makes us happy or suffer. This is how the untrained mind behaves, feeling the painful experience again and again." She likened it to the person who is resentful that someone brought her half a glass of water rather than focusing on the fact that the glass is half full. "We should be happy enough to be alive. Instead of complaining, be joyful. Learn from the body not to carry heavy things, and you will find that happiness is present here and now. Please be a happy child of the Buddha."

Her point about choosing happiness rather than clinging to suffering was pretty simple, but the message resonated with me in a new way. I thought about how I clung to my resentments with Randall. It had been eight months since surgery. I conjured up the memory. *How could he abandon me like that?* Still angry, I felt like a prisoner dragging a ball and chain of pain and resentment behind me. Maybe it was time to let go. But letting go involved forgiveness, and I wasn't ready for that yet. I preferred to wallow in my misery and blame him, rather than take responsibility for changing my attitude.

Perhaps Dhammananda could help me learn to let go, to release old hurts. It wasn't just my husband. I still carried painful memories from childhood, as if they were precious cargo that I couldn't bear to part with. I had a penchant for focusing on the glass being half empty, holding on to suffering as if it were my only option. I had no idea how to let go but was willing to explore new possibilities.

After her talk the crowd began to pass eight brand-new saffron robes packaged in plastic wrap from the back of the room. People blessed the robe, holding it to their forehead before passing it on to the person in the next row. Eventually it traveled forward until it reached the front where Dhammananda sat. The nuns recited special blessings over the robes. At the end of the ceremony Dhammananda dipped a handful of soft sticks that looked like straw into an ornamental gold bowl filled with water. She made her way slowly down the length of the hall, flinging water on people's heads and reciting a blessing as she went. When she approached me, I felt the cool drops against my face. I didn't understand the words she was saying, but I felt an intimate connection to everyone around me. We lowered our heads and pressed our palms together close to our hearts. I was one body among many, warm and peaceful, humbled to be part of the community that surrounded me. That's why I loved coming to the temple. I'd finally found a place that felt like home, a place where I belonged.

By mid-afternoon, after a light lunch in the dining area, most of the crowd had left the temple. I knew Dhammananda had met individually with people after lunch and wondered if she would be too tired to speak to me. I found her in the office where she was working on her computer. She was wearing a long, buttoned-down, saffron-colored tunic with a mandarin collar that lay flat against her neck. When I walked in, she looked up, smiled, and pointed to the chair on the other side of her desk.

"How did you like the robes offering ceremony?"

"Beautiful—and so many people!"

"You have more questions for me?"

"What was the water that you sprinkled over people's heads?"

"It is holy water that has been blessed. I sprinkle it over them to wish them well and to thank them for bringing the robes for us."

I felt compelled to tell Dhammananda that I saw in myself the propensity to see the glass half empty. She had a story at the ready for me:

"Today a woman came to the temple. The woman was upset because she'd had an accident in front of the temple. I told her that is good, rather than somewhere else where there would be no one to help her. She said the cost of fixing her car was about 100,000 baht ($3,000). I said that's well and good. Better it happened at the temple. Then she asked for forgiveness for coming with red hair. I spoke very directly to her because I consider her like a daughter. If it is someone else's head that is pink, blue, purple, whatever, I don't care. But I care because she is like my daughter. So much good work she has done for the temple. May this merit go first to her, then to the deva who is protecting her, and also to those she has transgressed. May they also come and share with her this good merit, may they forgive her. May she be happy, and may they be happy. People around her, parents, family members, may they also rejoice in this merit-making that she has done. If you know how to collect the merit around you, then your mind rejoices. This is how to make our lives joyful, sometimes you didn't even have to do it yourself."

I felt confused, not sure how to interpret this story or how it related to me. Sometimes Dhammananda told anecdotes that seemed like parables, and I had to decipher their meaning. I gathered it annoyed her that this young woman had dyed her hair red. Still, the main point of the story seemed to be about collecting merit. I knew the Thai definition of making merit is doing positive good for others in the world. By collecting merit, she was instructing me to rejoice in people's acts of kindness, celebrate that which is positive, and not dwell on the negative. Of course, dwelling on the negative was my forte. I even had a nickname for myself, "Queen of the Dark Side." Dhammananda knew I was struggling to change my attitude, so I sought her advice.

"I have a hard time seeing the positive. My mind is so dark," I said.

"Blocked, blocked. You don't see." She paused as if she were talking to a flower on a nearby tree. "Look at this flower, so beautiful. I have not seen you before. Look at the young leaf coming up. How beautiful is life? Or someone is making something beautiful, so you rejoice. There are so many ways of keeping our lives joyful. Sometimes I check on my leaves and flowers. Oh! I have not seen you before. Thank you. Thank you. So, every day you are picking up merit, somebody else is making it, but you are also sharing it. This is how to make our life blossom, joyful. So much good energy, and when you feel that your face blossoms. That Cindy, she has so much good energy, I can feel it when I talk to her."

I smiled, reveling in her words.

"The Buddha says things must change. We have suffered for so long. We are changing for the better."

It was easy in this moment to confide in her that I no longer felt fulfilled by my role as caretaker to my husband and son. I even confessed to feeling a bit lonely, unsure of myself.

"Sometimes I feel lost," I said. "Like I no longer recognize myself in the mirror. It's like the old Cindy has vanished, and all that remains is an empty shell." I wondered if Dhammananda had ever questioned herself; she seemed so confident and strong. "Can you tell me a time when you struggled or questioned yourself?"

Dhammananda shifted forward in her seat. Her face seemed to soften as if she were lost in thought. "In 1981 I had a midlife crisis. I was thirty-seven. I could hardly eat. My life was completely meaningless. I was married with three boys and had a successful academic career, yet I felt worthless and empty inside. On weekends, I would meditate with my mother, hidden in the back, crying. Something was missing. Being a wife, mother, and professor wasn't enough anymore."

She looked pensive as she said, "I retreated into a back room and started to draw, simple line sketches. My boys would sneak into the room, quietly peer over my shoulder, and ask me what I was doing. 'Drawing,' I told them. I explained my drawings to them, and they encouraged me to write captions for each sketch so that others could understand. Eventually I collected enough drawings to publish a book. It became a top seller in 1983."

I was amazed that out of her suffering Dhammananda had managed to create something beautiful for others. I was about to ask her if she still had a copy of the book when we heard the gong ring. *Tong-tong-tong.*

Dhammananda turned to look at the clock on the wall behind her. "Look at the time!" Dhammananda exclaimed. "Four o'clock. Now we go work in the garden. Come!"

Caught off guard, I jumped at the sound of the gong. I didn't like that our conversation had been cut short. Undeterred by the interruption, Dhammananda gathered her robes and headed out the door. I stuffed my notes into a bag and scrambled to catch up with her. Outside, all the nuns were gathered at the front wall of the temple. There was a rocky mound of earth near the right corner of the fence that Dhammananda wanted removed and transferred to the back of the garden.

How stupid, I thought, my resentment growing. *We're moving dirt from one space to another.* The task at hand seemed senseless, and it was replacing my one-on-one time with Dhammananda. *Why do I have to do this?* It was hot, and I was already dripping with sweat. Women lifted hoes and pickaxes, chipping away at the dirt mound, inching their way forward bit by bit, and leaving chunks of semi-dry earth and rocks. Several of us moved in with shovels and plastic buckets to haul the debris away. We stood side by side, passing the buckets hand over hand until they reached the last person in line who dumped the contents into a large wheelbarrow. We looked like buzzing bees fluttering around.

Just then Dhammananda stepped forward, hoe in hand. She hoisted the hoe above her and with the entire force of her upper body swung it down. For her age, she was remarkably strong. It dawned on me that this was the true nature of her determination, the drive behind her formidable decision to walk the path as the lone Theravada nun. Just like her mother, she was a force to be reckoned with, even though at times her kind manner and calm speech belied the fire in her belly. Impressed, I no longer questioned the rhyme or reason of the manual work; I simply joined in with the others. We laughed and enjoyed ourselves. I discovered that it doesn't matter what the task at hand is, just be present and willing, and reap the benefits of physical labor.

We worked for an hour and drank cool water distributed at the end. The evening air was cool against my sweaty face. I thought about Dhammananda's earlier Dhamma talk, how we cling to our resentments and focus on our disappointments. I pictured myself angry—hot and frustrated with steam pouring out of my ears. I had grown up thinking anger was a bad thing and stuffed it inside. But stuffing it down only resulted in a huge explosion like hot lava flowing from a volcano. Occasionally I would end up blowing my top, spewing resentment and vitriol and afterwards regretting it. Resentment in itself isn't wrong, but the broader question is, what purpose does it serve? If harnessed properly, anger can be a powerful motivator for positive change. I couldn't help but remember the mighty swing Dhammananda took as she slammed that hoe into the hard earth, knocking it to pieces. I wondered if part of her strength and resolve had been born from seeds of anger. I had no way of knowing, but I did remember what she said that first time I heard her speak. "Anger doesn't lead us anywhere. It is more difficult to practice compassion and loving kindness. That is the goal of Buddhism." I had a lot to learn about transforming my anger into a positive force for good. I wasn't there yet, but with Dhammananda's help, maybe I could learn.

On the ride home from the temple, I observed the soot-covered buildings outside my window. I marveled that it had been almost a year since we'd moved to Thailand. During that time, my son had started a brand-new school, and my husband had launched into a new job. I'd confronted a major back problem, had surgery, and begun an intensive recovery process. It would take years before I fully understood the degree to which my time in Thailand catapulted me into a spiritual journey. I did understand, however, that were it not for my back injury, I never would have embarked on that journey in the first place. It's true what they say, that blessings are born out of suffering. My desire to heal led me to the temple and the discovery of my beloved teacher, Dhammananda.

When my physical decline began, it seemed to me that the universe was confirming my worst childhood fear: pain equals punishment. I must have done something wrong, just like my mom said; otherwise, why would I be hurting so much? I felt helpless, and on top of that, it was probably my own fault. It would take another several years to cultivate a new perspective—that my back injury was not punishment, but the beginning of a healing process.

My back injury forced me to come to a complete halt. Having no external distractions, I focused inward, on myself. The surgery and recovery process were like walking a labyrinth. I entered through the physical portal, which eventually led to emotional and spiritual passageways.

As we wound our way back home, I thought back to the previous December, a month before surgery. I could visualize myself out on the front porch, seated in the rocking chair, swaying back and forth, looking out at the surrounding tropical forest. The mass of tangled vines wrapped around tree trunks reminded me of my jangled insides—scared, helpless, and hurting. I breathed a heavy sigh in the back seat, pushing that painful memory aside.

But the thoughts kept coming like a waterfall cascading down. A strong backbone signified the measure of a person's strength; it was the body's internal support system, and mine was weak and degenerative. It was probably no accident that my internal scaffolding was crumbling. The foundation of my very being was in question. In retrospect, I was a wreck, unable to support myself physically, emotionally, or spiritually. I needed to mend myself from the inside out, and I needed help.

First, I had to reconstruct my spine, which I did through the surgery and two titanium discs implanted in my lower back. All my life, my back had been the repository of unexpressed feelings from childhood. Over the years, tension and stress had accumulated there. In Thailand, I had the support I needed to rest, recuperate, and build up my strength once again.

Next, I needed the emotional support of a loving mother figure who, through her unconditional love, would lead me on a path of self-acceptance. I had to discover how to take care of myself in ways I had never learned growing up. I had always thought I needed to be there to provide emotional support for my parents, and this extended into adulthood with my husband. I measured my self-worth according to my ability to support others. My lower back was like a sponge, sucking up other people's troubles as if they were my own, a heavy burden to carry over a lifetime. I imagined that buildup of tension eventually caused distress in my lower spine. Thankfully in Thailand, I was able to begin healing my back and restoring my strength over time.

Outside I caught a glimpse of a store with Buddha statues lined in rows, golden and sparkling in the sun. The Buddhas' expressions conveyed a peaceful presence. I loved living in Thailand. *How lucky am I?* I thought.

I considered Durga, who provided me the physical and emotional support I needed at home to heal. She was my champion. From the moment I pulled into the driveway after my return flight from Munich, she'd stood by my side.

I remembered her waiting at the front door for me, smiling. She'd adorned the entryway with two clay elephants with yellow wreaths of marigolds draped over their necks.

As we approached the house, I was eager to see her and affirm our connection. As soon as I opened the car door, Durga rushed up to my side. "I help you, madam." I was exhausted, and let myself press against her—my arm on her arm—and leaned into her as we took those first few steps together. She never left me unattended. Watching me closely, she guided me to a chair in the living room, stacking pillows around me in a pool of softness. Durga—a pillar of strength for me to rely on.

Durga was a teacher for me. She was kind and compassionate, strong yet yielding in her unselfish concern for others. I had always been afraid of giving myself fully to others because it meant self-sacrifice, but Durga didn't appear to be diminished by her caring for others. On the contrary, she seemed satisfied and happy with her life. She reminded me of a little Buddha. There was a glow about her, an internal light that radiated from her eyes.

Healing, of necessity, required faith, and my faith grew as I prayed to the Medicine Buddha and spent time with Dhammananda. Without faith, we flounder and question the why behind every action. We try to find a reasonable explanation for the pain when there is none. Every so often, we realize that we are not in charge. We hold onto resentments and blame someone else as if they were responsible for our suffering. When we simply adjust our attitude and let go of blame, healing occurs naturally. We just need to let go and let ourselves receive the blessings we deserve. That day, between the Dhamma talk, the one-on-one conversation, and the work in the garden, I learned that surrendering requires faith, and that if I let go of resentments, I was on the right path.

Durga Praying. Photograph taken by
Nancy Zarider, April 2008.

Chapter 8:

Mother Love

The time I spent with Dhammananda was bringing up memories of my mother—all that she was and was not, the ways she'd failed me, and the ways she'd tried to be the best mother she could. As a child, I yearned for my mother's love but felt conflicted. On the one hand, I wanted her attention, while on the other, I was wary of her, never knowing what to expect. Her temper could flare erratically, and it was confusing to me because I felt ashamed when she got upset, often not understanding what I'd done to set her off.

I remember when I was four years old, home alone with my mother because my older sister was in school. I could feel her shadowy presence in the house. I wanted her to play with me, but she had other things on her mind. She would retire to the living room to read, or to sew in the den, while I kept myself company in my bedroom at the other end of the house playing with my Lincoln Logs. The year was 1955 and we were living in South Carolina. Our house was painted dark green, sequestered on a quiet street, surrounded by deep lush woods. One day I asked her if I could go outside to play.

"Mom, can I go to Sand River with Bonnie?"

"Did you put away your Lincoln Logs like I asked you to?"

"Yes, Mom." I made sure to clean up because I wanted her to say I could go.

"Sure, take a walk."

I put on my six-gun Davy Crockett holster, cowboy hat, and vest, and walked with my German Shepherd dog. Bonnie was a loving dog, black and brown with pointy ears, whose back reached up to my waist. A gentle dog, I called her.

"Come on Bonnie. Let's go to Sand River."

We headed down the dirt path covered with leaves behind our house. Along the way I picked fresh honeysuckle. I bit off the tip and sucked the sweet nectar inside. Bonnie ran ahead of me chasing birds and barking at the squirrels. We wound our way around to my secret hiding place. Sand River was an open spot in the woods with white sand. My mom said it was white because there was once a river there. I lay down in the sand. I loved the feeling of sifting sand through my fingers. Bonnie resting by my side, her warm body pressed against mine. When I got hungry I wandered back to the house.

I found my mom sitting in the living room reading, deep in thought. I gingerly approached her because I never knew how she'd respond.

"Mom, when is lunch?"

"Can't you see I'm busy? I'll call you when it's ready."

A complicated woman, my mom was a force to be reckoned with. Our family rabbi described my mother perfectly at her burial ceremony. "Katie was an inspiration to her children and to the many women who aspired to be like her." An attorney who'd graduated at the top of her law school class, she was ahead of her time. Most women never even considered having a professional career, but my mom was determined to achieve success in what was then a male-dominated field. She valued rational thought and practicality over what she considered the sentimental world of feelings.

When I got old enough to go to school, I would brag about her to my friends. I thought she was better and smarter than all the other moms. But secretly, I wished she would bake chocolate chip cookies and make sock puppets instead of always having her nose buried in a book.

I was proud of my mom and wanted to impress her, but I never felt I measured up. A thoughtful child, I wanted her to understand my sensitive feelings. Unfortunately, she was never able to provide that support. My favorite childhood story was *The Story of Ferdinand*. I fancied being out in the open field like Ferdinand, contemplating the beauty, smelling the flowers, taking my time. She preferred the masculine world of striving and competition, asserting her will, and defending her positions at all times. It was never okay to challenge her or to try to convince her otherwise.

As an adult, I look back on my childhood and wonder why I was left on my own at such a tender young age. Even though I longed for my mother's attention and caring, those nurturing qualities simply weren't part of her personality. Perhaps that's why, as an adult, I had such fear of being alone. I carried a reservoir of memories that equated being alone with abandonment and rejection. Ironically, I became more like my mother and learned to be stoic about my pain. I closed down like a clamshell, shutting down my vulnerable feelings to protect myself. Beneath that vulnerability was a powerful anger. Over the years, my resentment smoldered like burning embers, eating away at my insides until my teen years, when the embers caught fire and started to burn out of control.

My world changed dramatically when I was nine; my father was transferred from his job in South Carolina to Southern California. The move was traumatic for me. I had loved the tiny town of Aiken, where my best friend, Margie, and I would take off on our bikes and ride everywhere together. On Saturdays we could see a movie for a quarter. There were two theaters in town, the Annabel Lee and the Rosemarie. After a movie, we'd stop by the Woolworth's to sit at the soda counter. For a nickel you could buy a balloon, pop it, and see if you were lucky enough to win the prize inside, noted on a tag that read, "Free hot fudge sundae." Once, during a hurricane, Margie and I sat in the basement, lit candles, and read *Nancy Drew* mysteries all night. We were inseparable. Leaving Margie was hard enough, but leaving behind my beloved dog, Bonnie, was intolerable.

"Why can't we take Bonnie?" I pleaded with my mother.

"We can't travel across the country in our Chevy station wagon with a dog. We just barely fit everyone and everything into the car. The answer is no." She refused to be swayed, no matter how hard I begged. I couldn't understand why my mom was so strict, but whenever she made a decision, she stuck firmly to it. It was as if I were invisible to her, and my feelings didn't matter. I left the South with a broken heart and feeling utterly alone. This may have been the first time I experienced depression, although I didn't have a name for what I was feeling at the time. It just seemed like a dark cloud had enveloped me, and I was sad with little or no interest in our new surroundings.

I must have been angry with my mother, but didn't have a way to make sense of these deep wounds at the time. In third grade at my new school in Southern California, the teacher assigned a project to the class to write a book. Mine was called *The Little Flame that Grew.* The flame was a friendly source of comfort to me at the time. Bright red, the flame had expressive eyes and a bright smile. Looking back on it, though, I wonder if this was my nascent anger trying to express itself.

As difficult as my mother was, I longed to be close to her. Since I didn't feel that connection, I created an elaborate fantasy in my mind. I must have been eight or nine at the time, when Barbie dolls were popular. I imagined my mom and me as a blond mother-daughter team who spent hours together brushing and shaping our hair. Blond Mom walked around in high heels and wore sparkly dresses. We were always smiling and standing close to each other. The truth was that my mom and I both had dark brown hair; she preferred pants to dresses, and high heels were not her style. It was a challenge to be close to someone so independent.

I wondered if my sister ever felt a lack of caring from my mom. I don't know, since we never discussed it. By the time we moved to California, Ellie was already in junior high school. We shared a room, just as we had in South Carolina, but we weren't as close as we had been. In South Carolina we'd played together and confided in one another. After we moved to California, my sister developed a close network of girlfriends outside the home. I suppose it had something to do with her age; she was thirteen and I was nine. She became more involved in her social group, which is appropriate for a teenager. Still, it only accentuated my feelings of being left behind.

Ellie was perfect in my mother's eyes—the one she preferred, or so it seemed. I never heard my mom yell at my sister or tell her what to do. Unlike my sister, who was short and petite, I was chunky and solid and felt self-conscious about my size. As far as I could tell, Ellie could do no wrong. She always seemed happy and outgoing, with lots of friends. I usually had one close friend at a time and was shy and withdrawn. I imagined if I were thinner, more outgoing, and popular like my sister, my mom would love me more. This was my childhood dilemma, never feeling good enough, but trying to be perfect on the off chance I could win my mother's love.

Despite my difficulties with my mother, there were a couple of bright spots in our relationship. She had a creative side, and sharing it with me brought us together. Her two passions in life were her love of good food and her love of dance—both of which she introduced me to at a young age. When Jewish holidays came around, we spent time together in the kitchen making *mandelbrot*, a twice-baked cookie kind of like biscotti. She saw that I loved baking and bought me Duncan Hines cake mixes. She even taught me how to make boiled icing. I felt connected to my mom in these moments and was proud of my creations.

She had a special fondness for dance. Her face would light up when she talked about doing tap and ballet as a young woman. She giggled like a child when we asked her to show us "the old soft shoe," tapping her toes and shuffling from one foot to the other. My mom helped me survive the move to Los Angeles by enrolling me in my first dance class—which opened up a whole new world to me that would continue throughout my life.

My first teacher, Sheila Rozann, was the quintessential ballerina, dressed in a V-necked pink leotard, pink tights, and a soft chiffon skirt that wrapped and tied in front. She wore a lot of makeup and spoke with a funny accent. I idolized her. She had exotic brown eyes and brown hair done up in a bouffant. A gifted teacher, she was passionate about dance. I knew that Ms. Rozann expected me to work hard and give it my all, and I did. I still dream about that little studio in Chatsworth, a rectangular space with mirrors covering the front wall, a double set of barres that wrapped around the room, and in one corner a pianist who played live musical accompaniment.

When I stepped into that room, it was like crossing over into a sacred realm—one where I could relax, pause, and fully embody the joy of my body moving in time to the music.

I took class three days a week, twice after school and once on Saturday morning. The ritual began in the dressing room. I would take off my street clothes and pull on pink tights first, then a black cotton leotard, and finally put on soft, pink ballet slippers. I loved those shoes, soft leather that fit my feet snuggly. Entering the dance room was like entering a sacred space. All the chatter dissipated when Ms. Rozann walked in. From then on, it was only the shuffle of feet and the music. I never felt alone in dance class. Moving in unison with the group was sharing an intimate connection with others, not through words, but through movement.

The first half of class we warmed up at the barre. I liked doing arabesque with my back leg extended behind me. Discovering how to balance took patience. My mind became calm as my focus turned inward. If I caught my balance just right, it felt effortless, like flying in the air, weightless. I loved being perched in that position.

The second half of class we moved to the center of the room to do floor routines.

I liked the sensations of moving. Spreading my arms in second position, lifting off the ground in light jetés. We did simple jumps in place, landing with the right foot forward, then switching in the air and landing with the left foot forward, back and forth sixteen times with my teacher clapping the rhythm. I felt each pulse in my body as I prepared for the jump, bending slightly before pushing my toes off the ground and leaping in the air. I wanted to jump high and long, never to return to earth if I could help it. It was the closest I ever came to the feeling of flying. Even earthbound, I was grateful my mom started me dancing so young.

The worst time of my life with my mom was when I was in high school. Our relationship deteriorated into constant shouting matches. She'd start in on me with a familiar refrain like, "Didn't I ask you to clean the living room?" This was the signal the fight was about to begin. She'd keep at me until she'd fly off the handle and start yelling.

"Do it now, or I won't let you go out tonight."

I felt a silent scream welling up inside. One day I let it go.

"I hate you! Stop ordering me around! Why can't you leave me alone?"

"Don't yell at me. I'm your mother. Do what I say!" She had to have the last word; it always ended the same.

It was futile to argue with her. There was no chance I'd win. She would stick to her position, even when it didn't make any sense. Our constant shouting matches left me numb. I pretended to hang tough until I reached my room, but there my shoulders would collapse. I'd fall on to my bed feeling hopeless and defeated, arms crossed behind my head, staring at the ceiling.

When I turned seventeen, the last semester of my junior year, my father was transferred again from Southern California to Northern California. Throughout high school, I had dreamed of being a varsity cheerleader during fall football season. During the spring track season I was elected cheerleader, so I thought my chances of being re-elected in the fall were pretty good. Thanks to my dance background, I was skilled at mastering complicated routines. Students cheered me on as I swirled, kicked high, and did the splits. This was my one chance to be popular like my sister, who had also been a cheerleader. Quiet and studious, I longed for that recognition.

My mother insisted that I move. I begged her to let me stay behind and live with my best friend, Eileen Acos, nicknamed "the Greek," whose parents had invited me to stay with them. I screamed and cried to no avail. "Why don't you let me live with Eileen?"

"The answer is no and that's final." She didn't give me a reason. Like a boulder, my mother remained stolid, unshaken in her position. She decided I had to leave, and that was all there was to it. Once again, my feelings didn't count. Looking back on that summer, I can see I descended into a dark cavern of isolation and depression. I began to lose confidence. My mother's inability to see me as a person, or to support my needs, left me feeling isolated and alone. I had no one to talk to, no one who could understand what I was going through. I was too young to know how to take care of myself, to love myself and accept that I needed help. If I felt any anger, it was trapped inside. I internalized my rage and directed my hatred back at myself. This marked the start of a full-blown depression. I had little energy and no desire to do anything; dark moods haunted me.

I suppose I was more resilient than I realized, although I felt helpless at the time. The one voice I did hear was, "I need to get out of here." I enrolled in summer school to finish the classes I needed to take in order to graduate from high school by the start of fall semester. In the meantime, I applied to UC Riverside six weeks before school started on the off chance that I might be accepted. I received my high school diploma at the end of the summer, and UC Riverside accepted me for the fall semester. A freshman at seventeen, I was relieved to be moving on. This resolved the immediate dilemma of how to escape my mother's wrath, but it didn't solve the inherent conflict in our relationship. Did my mother love me? Was I a worthy daughter? I didn't discover the answers for many years to come; however, my relationship with my mother did improve toward the end of her life.

In those final years, she became one of my most loyal advocates. We made peace as she aged. At eighty-five, she was still living alone in her own home. She had fallen several times and even passed out once while she was driving. I became concerned and asked if I could talk to her doctor. I remember being shocked when I heard him say, "Your mother is too old to be living alone; she needs to be closer to family." I had always thought of my mother as fiercely independent. Now I had to adjust to the reality that my mom needed my help. She moved into an assisted living facility nearby. After thirty years of living separately, I had the chance to get to know my mother again. I wanted to see if we could be friends.

We saw each other every week, went to the movies, and shared all the major holidays together. Even though I wrestled with our relationship when I was young, as an adult, we found a way to coexist. I loved her and she loved me. I came to appreciate her stubborn tenacity as the will to persevere, a quality I admired and one that I share.

I cared a lot about her and treated her with kindness, grateful for our connection. After she passed, I missed her companionship and those daily phone calls. Even though we had become closer, I still carried deep scars from childhood and unresolved resentment toward her. I had internalized my mother's rejection and, just as she had been unable to love me, I was incapable of loving myself. I was my own worst enemy, criticizing myself and ignoring my wants and needs.

Dhammananda was the first woman to show me unconditional love—something my mom wasn't able to give me. Sitting with her felt like being wrapped in angel's wings that comforted and held me. With her tender gaze, Dhammananda expressed her complete acceptance of me just as I was. I felt like a young child in her presence, soaking up her love.

Dhammananda often said that, in order to heal ourselves, we must heal the mother-daughter relationship. I hadn't realized it at the time, but as Dhammananda and I spent more time together, I became like a daughter to her and she a mother to me. She wanted me to begin to see the beauty that surrounded me and not focus on the dark, painful memories of the past. Through her unconditional love, she was providing me with the emotional and spiritual road map to begin to forgive my mother and learn to love myself. Although I still carried resentment, I began to understand that, with time and practice, I might be able to view myself through a more compassionate lens. As I spent time with Dhammananda, she guided me along a path of embracing my womanhood and healing the resentments buried deep within.

Chapter 9:

The Healing Circle

Dhammananda and I met again in December of 2006 when I returned to join the nuns for the full moon ceremony. As we drove through the temple gates, I felt a familiar sense of relief and excitement to be leaving my normal routine behind. Returning to the temple was like coming home to a safe place.

Stepping out of the car, I cast a glance at my shadow, the black silhouette of a willing pilgrim who longed to walk alongside her teacher in search of a spiritual connection. I recalled the nervousness I'd felt the first time I visited the temple. This time I felt excited, but not scared. I still needed more information to write my article, but realized that after today's interview, I would have what I needed. Although writing the piece had been my original pretext for meeting with Dhammananda, I had seen early on that what I really wanted was a close relationship with a woman I deeply admired. Each time we met, our bond became stronger. By this time, our fourth interview, our talks were becoming more intimate; we were fond of each other.

I walked to the open dining area, shielded from the blistering, mid-afternoon sun by the roof overhead. Dhammananda was seated at a metal table. A woman stood behind her massaging her head and digging her fingers into her scalp. Dhammananda waved her hand, signaling for me to join them. She closed her eyes and let out a long sigh as she soaked up each stroke. When the massage was finished, I asked Dhammananda, "Isn't it unusual for someone to be touching your head?"

She reached back and patted the hands of the woman standing behind her. "I only let very close friends touch me." She grimaced and said, "Westerners always grab me on the shoulder." Then she playfully wrapped her friend's arm around her shoulder. "And I have to slowly move their arm away, because they really shouldn't be touching me."

She turned around and looked at her friend. "This is Khun Pao. I met her while teaching Buddhist Studies at Thammasat University. She was an engineer for the Thai army, doing chemical research." She told me that General Pao, now retired, traveled by bus from Bangkok, over an hour's journey, three days a week to learn English from Dhammananda.

Dhammananda turned to take Khun Pao's hand and spoke in English.

"Cindy is writing an article about me. She always comes with a list of questions. Let's go into my office where it is quiet. Come." Dhammananda gestured. We walked over together. She took a seat behind her desk, and I sat across from her.

"Okay if I record our conversation?"

"Sure." She always agreed, but it felt better to ask permission. When I flipped on the digital device, a buzz of excitement spread through me. I always looked forward to our time together. As I sat in her presence, I felt special, as if I had stepped out of the dark shadows into the light. She seemed to delight in regaling me with her stories, and I was full of anticipation, eager to hear more. I shuffled through my papers until I found my list of questions.

"Last time we met, you spoke about having a midlife crisis. That was 1981. In 2001, twenty years later, you became a *sameneri*. I am curious to know how you arrived at your decision to be ordained. Can you tell me more about that?"

"It was 1999, before the new millennium." Dhammananda traced the desk with her index finger. "I wanted to do something memorable with my life." She explained that she had taken a workshop in which she was asked to draw a river. The river was like a depiction of her life. She had drawn red flags to mark any significant events and hopes for the future. She knew she wanted to take the bodhisattva's vows in 2000, and drew a flag to represent that. She leaned forward in her chair and said there were two other things.

"First, I wanted to be celibate. That may sound strange. I was a married woman with a family, but it's true. Second, I wanted to be vegetarian. That wasn't so strange because my mother had been a vegetarian since I was ten."

When Dhammananda took the bodhisattva vows in April 2000, she fulfilled her commitments to be vegetarian and celibate. Those commitments coincided with divorcing her husband. She explained that taking the vows signified the beginning of her decision to enter the spiritual path. It wasn't until the end of the year that she decided to be ordained as a sameneri.

I tried to picture Dhammananda before she was ordained—before she had shaved her head or put on her robes. Wondering out loud, I asked her, "What was your lay life like?"

She replied emphatically, "I was an academic, a professor of Buddhist Studies for twenty-seven years at Thammasat

University before I resigned my position. I was a respected Buddhist scholar, well known at the peak of my professional career. I co-founded and directed the India Studies Department for four years and loved that." I could see Dhammananda was a woman who, no matter what she chose to do in her life, jumped in with both feet and never hesitated. Her determination and confidence were two qualities I admired. She didn't appear conceited in describing her past accomplishments, only genuinely proud of herself.

Listening to her made me realize that I was not good at taking credit for my own accomplishments. When people complimented me, I would brush it off or minimize it by thinking, *I don't really believe them; they must be saying that just to be nice to me. If they knew the real Cindy, they would see what an imposter I am.* A perfectionist, I was my own worst critic. *Not good enough,* I would tell myself. Dhammananda's confidence inspired me to adopt a new perspective. Maybe I wasn't perfect, but I could at least begin to give myself the benefit of the doubt by admitting that, in most situations, I had tried my best. Even though I was not good at acknowledging myself, I resolved to do better.

Dhammananda gathered her robes and adjusted one end over her shoulder. "Seven years before my ordination, I was the host of a popular TV show." She paused briefly before continuing. "I need to give you the historical context. In 1993 there was a monk scandal in the country that lasted for more than a year before the sangha made the decision to disrobe the monk." She explained that there had been a TV show that focused on the scandal. The producers invited four women, including Dhammananda, to discuss the issue. Although I was curious to know what the scandal was about, she didn't mention it, and I decided not to interrupt her for fear of losing the thread of the conversation.

Dhammananda said she was asked to appear on the program since she was a well-respected Buddhist scholar. The show was very popular, and Dhammananda was thrown into the spotlight overnight.

She smiled as she recalled the experience. "I'd accepted the invitation right away, thinking all along I would appear in just that one episode. I didn't understand that they wanted me to host the program moving forward." She told me that before each show she spent a long time on her hair, makeup, painting her nails, and choosing her clothes. She was proud of the fact that in its last two years, the show won the award for best Dhamma TV talk show.

Dhammananda paused to take a sip of tea. It wasn't hard to visualize her as a popular professor and TV host. She was a dynamic speaker and came alive before an audience. Having accomplished so much, I couldn't imagine how Dhammananda—at the peak of her career—decided to give it all up. Not only that, Dhammananda also made huge changes in her personal life by divorcing her husband and leaving her adult sons to care for themselves. I thought it was courageous that she didn't feel obliged to stay in her marriage out of guilt or responsibility to her husband. The truest part of her wanted to be more than just a wife and mother. It struck a resonant cord in me that I couldn't have articulated at the time, but it was reverberating through me nevertheless: I secretly desired to do what Dhammananda had done, to renounce my responsibilities as a wife and mother. But that would have meant leaving the comfort of my marriage, something I was not ready for. I was afraid to be on my own. Also, I wasn't ready to leave my fourteen-year-old son; he was still so young.

Dhammananda was a role model for me. Despite any fears or doubts she may have felt at the time, she remained true to herself. She risked losing everything in search of a more meaningful life. I wondered if I would be capable of doing the same. Unless I was willing to let go, I would never find out.

"With all you had accomplished, how did you decide to become a nun?" I asked.

"When the time came, it came. It started not with the interest in the ordained life, but with the dissatisfaction with worldly life. I had just finished doing my makeup for the TV program. I looked at my own reflection in the mirror, studied my face, and asked myself, *How long is this going to go on—putting on makeup, buying jewelry, dressing up in matching outfits?* It was quite sudden. I felt I had enough of dressing up, painting my face—and that is the moment when I made the decision to be ordained."

I fingered my own dyed, reddish-brown, shoulder length hair and felt a shiver of excitement go up my spine. Part of me was curious as to what I would look like with my head shaved. Dhammananda was so beautiful. I marveled at how her skin glowed and her eyes seemed to smile in delight. Whatever difficulties she may have gone through at the time she was ordained, leaving her family and her academic career, she had clearly made peace with her decision.

I could have gone on all day with her, but I knew our time was coming to an end so I asked one final question. I had heard from the other nuns that Dhammananda had been treated horribly on her return to Thailand from Sri Lanka, newly ordained. She was ostracized in the media. I was curious to know what she would say about her experience, so I asked her. "What was it like when you returned from Sri Lanka? How did people in Thailand react to your ordination?"

Dhammananda explained that the first three months after her ordination she became a victim of the media. "I received hate mail and nasty email messages." Dhammananda swept her hand across the desk as if she were wiping that memory aside. She said that her ordination stirred up a lot of controversy and talked about a particular radio talk show hosted by a former monk. The host asked people to phone in and comment about Dhammananda's situation, but he only recorded the negative comments and played them over and over again. He made it seem like everyone opposed the issue of women's ordination. She looked at me and said, "I didn't read the Thai newspapers for two years because the media campaign against me was so strong." I often saw her reading the newspaper after lunch, and I couldn't imagine her not reading the news for two years. She must have felt really isolated and alone—especially as there were no other Thai bhikkhunis for her to turn to for support. I was just about to ask her if she felt lonely when she pushed her chair back and stood up.

"Now I must go attend to temple business. You take your dinner at five o'clock, and then we meet for the full moon celebration at seven." As usual, there was no formal ending to our meeting; she simply acknowledged that it was time for her to go. I bowed and thanked her. I wasn't ready for the interview to end. I cherished our time together and couldn't wait to get back to the room to replay the recording. I always heard more the second time I listened to our conversation.

I was staying in the cottage across the road from Dhammananda's main residence. It was the same cottage where I had stayed during my first visit to the temple, and where Dhammananda had written many of her books when she was a professor. I felt it was no coincidence that, once again, I had been assigned this room. Like Dhammananda, I aspired to be a writer. Feeling the energy of the guesthouse and knowing she had written there, provided me with inspiration to follow my teacher's example and put my pen to paper.

Later that evening, we gathered for chanting and meditation on the second floor of the main prayer hall. There were fourteen women in the group. The two ordained women knelt in the front row, and Dhammananda sat to their right. Six maejis knelt on the mats behind the nuns, and in the third row were six laywomen, including me. I took a seat in back next to a young Thai woman who held in her hands a framed picture under glass of the Medicine Buddha. The dark blue Buddha wore a gold robe and was seated on a lotus blossom with pink petals and green leaves that floated on a light blue lake with rolling hills in the foreground. A red halo shrouded the deity's head, and white clouds hovered above him. In his right hand he held a plant and in his left an alms bowl with a flowering plant growing from the top. The Thai woman stepped forward and presented the painting to Dhammananda who translated for me in English.

"This is a Tibetan *thangka* she brought for me to bless." The nuns began chanting, and Dhammananda closed her eyes and moved her lips silently. She then dipped her fingertips in a white paste and tapped the painting with six white dots in the shape of a small triangle at the bottom edge. She later told me that the white dots signified that the thangka had received the ritual blessing.

After the chanting, Dhammananda announced in English, "Now we will go to the back garden and recite the Medicine Buddha chant." I was touched with how often she translated for me in English, taking a personal interest in making sure I understood what was happening. Dhammananda walked briskly out of the room. We followed in silence behind her to the Medicine Buddha, who was no longer in the same place where I had originally seen him. He had been moved to the site where the future vihara would be constructed around him. He was still covered up and would remain so until the unveiling ceremony and the completion of the vihara, which would take another year and a half. We sat at the base of the structure in white plastic chairs divided into two groups. The maejis and ordained women sat on one side, and the laywomen on the other.

Dhammananda began by chanting the Medicine Buddha prayer, and then each group took turns reciting it. As soon as one group finished, the other group would begin. It went back and forth like this for what seemed like quite a long time. Even though I knew the prayer by heart, the words spun by so fast I couldn't keep up. Unsettled, I felt like I was in the middle of a race but falling behind. The chants began to sound like drum beats pounding back and forth in my ears. We recited the prayer so many times I lost count, until the voices suddenly stopped and there was an abrupt silence.

Dhammananda asked us to move our chairs into a circle and invited each one of us to talk about our day. She often encouraged sharing after evening meditation. There was lots of laughing and giggling as each woman took her turn. A quiet-mannered Thai woman with shoulder length brown hair who appeared to be in her twenties shared first. After she finished speaking, Dhammananda translated what she said into English.

"At lunchtime we celebrated this sister's birthday." She turned her gaze to the woman who had just spoken in Thai. "I surprised her with a gift I made for her. I embroidered a collar and managed to keep it a secret from everyone. She was delighted with my gift and the lunch of long noodles prepared especially for her." Dhammananda explained that these noodles are a symbol of long life that Thais prepare on birthdays. I was there at lunchtime, but hadn't realized that the noodles I'd eaten had a special significance. There were so many traditions and customs I wasn't aware of. I felt embarrassed, even a little ashamed that I had no idea there was a birthday celebration. I didn't even remember eating long noodles. I wanted to feel included, that I belonged, but there were many instances when I simply didn't have a clue what was going on. All I could do was admit that, for the moment, I felt like part of the group, and I knew that I would learn more as time went on.

As the woman sitting beside me shared, I began to feel nervous because I knew my turn was next. When it was time for me to speak, I glanced down to gather my thoughts before I opened my mouth. Speaking softly, I said, "I am so grateful. Everyone is so accepting of me. I feel like I belong here." Humbled, I paused in silence to look at the women's faces around the circle. As Dhammananda translated my words into Thai, they watched me intently. I admired these women. There were dedicated volunteers, cooking all day, cleaning, and completing whatever tasks needed to be done. Dressed in simple shorts, flip-flops, and plain T-shirts, they clearly relished Dhammananda's attention and took pride in their accomplishments. Just like me, they cherished her love. They even called her by a term of endearment, *Luang Mae*, meaning Venerable Mother.

As the other women shared in Thai, I drifted off deep in thought. I considered how I felt a mother-daughter connection to Dhammananda just like the other women. I'd felt this before, to be sure, but it was a revelation to realize I was not unique in this regard. Dhammananda's love was like an abundant fountain. She invited all of us to drink until we were satisfied. Unlike my own mother, Dhammananda had no scarcity of love. I didn't need to fight for her approval, be jealous of the others, cling to her, or compete for her attention, because she loved us all the same. It seemed there was nothing I could do or say to make her love me or the other women any less.

When the sharing drew to a close, a light rain began to fall as we headed back to our rooms. One woman with short clipped dark hair stepped next to me and linked her arm in mine. "Khun Cindy," she said with a smile. We giggled as tiny wet drops splashed our faces. In that moment I murmured to myself, *This is what it's like to come home, to feel the loving embrace of acceptance.*

It rained all night, and the wet grass cuttings stuck to my sandals as I crossed the lawn to the main prayer hall. Dhammananda didn't show up for morning chanting, so Dhammavanna led the procession up the stairs. At seven, when the gong rang for breakfast, Dhammananda strode into the dining area. While thoughtfully scooping spoonfuls of rice from her alms bowl, she read a magazine article. I finished eating breakfast and lingered at a nearby table. I wanted to ask a few more questions but hesitated, since I knew she would be traveling to South Korea later. I approached her table, bowed before her on my knees, and asked if she had time for a short conversation. She agreed to meet me in her office in fifteen minutes.

As I sat waiting outside her office, my eyes settled on the beautiful painting of Tara behind her desk. I was reminded of her youngest son, the artist who painted it for her. I had been thinking about the men in her life. I never asked about her father and how he influenced her, but I was curious to know whether she would be willing to talk about him.

Dhammananda soon joined me in the office. She set

down her cup of tea on the desk, and I took my usual seat across from her.

"Thank you for meeting with me," I said. "I have heard a lot about your mother but never discussed your father with you. Would you be willing to talk about him and how he influenced you?"

Dhammananda smiled, clearly delighted to be asked. "My father belonged to the south (Trang). His assets, his people, his context were all in the south. He was the first feminist I ever met." She threw her arms out wide. "He was a big, huge man, very hairy, typical of men who come from the south. He really liberated me from the traditional female stereotypes by encouraging me to do whatever I wanted. He gave me my own camera when I was twelve and taught me to play golf before it was popular in Thailand. He never let me get away with the excuse that I couldn't do something because I was a girl. He broke all the rules. When my mother came home and saw us playing cards or checkers, she said he was wasting our time."

Dhammananda explained that her father was a politician of the Democratic Party and a member of Parliament from Trang Province. The military leadership didn't like him for speaking out against the government, and he was imprisoned several times. He had a strong sense of social justice. Because of his political involvement, he remained in the south while Dhammananda's mother raised her children in Bangkok. Her mother moved to Bangkok when Dhammananda was five, which meant she only saw her father when Parliament was in session.

"I was always scared that he was going to be taken to jail," Dhammananda said. "Because I saw how much he went through, I completely shunned politics."

Then Dhammananda smiled. She was clearly fond of her

father. "He gave us both his wealth and his debts; there was no holding back. He was a joyful person with a loving heart. I inherited my sense of social responsibility from him and my commitment to the monastic lifestyle from my mother."

There was a long pause before she announced, "Now it's time for me to get ready for my trip."

I bowed and thanked her. I gathered up my belongings from my room and headed outside to wait for my driver who, as it turned out, was already parked in the front lot waiting for me. On the ride back to Bangkok, traffic was heavy, and we moved slowly. I was hot and tired, ready to take a warm shower and sleep in my own bed. I was reminded of what Dhammananda said: "Monastic life is not for everyone." Even so, I kept coming back. I always left feeling renewed, more at peace with myself.

As we drove past the gray, soot-covered buildings, I thought about the women's sharing circle, our relationship to Dhammananda, and our relationship to our mothers. So many women suffer from an absence of their mother's love. Dhammananda was helping us heal our childhood wounds. We were part of a larger healing circle of women, mending our hearts slowly, learning how to love ourselves, and practicing loving kindness with others. I felt grateful to be included.

On a personal level, my mother's neglect had haunted me. Even though we'd improved our relationship in later years, I always felt an inner emptiness, a hunger in my belly that could never be satisfied. I was always overeating as a child, as if food were a substitute for love. I felt ashamed because I tried to sneak extra servings when my mother wasn't looking. With Dhammananda I felt like a baby bird, mouth open, waiting to be nourished by her love. The secret, I realized as I looked out the car window at the landscape passing by, was to learn to nourish myself, but for now I would have to be content to rely on my teacher's example.

As my driver pulled up our driveway, my thoughts drifted back to Dhammananda's comment that women need to heal the mother-daughter relationship. I was not yet ready to forgive my mother, but trusted that, in time, I would be. A sweet feeling of happiness spread through me. As I let go of pain, I felt a glimmer of hope, and tears of gratitude slid down my cheeks. Dhammananda's love had kindled a spark of forgiveness in my heart—for my mother and for myself. That was the beauty of having a devoted teacher like Dhammananda who led me on a spiritual path of healing and happiness just by following her example.

Chapter 10:

Roots of My Own

The next few weeks leading into the holidays were busy. We traveled home to California over Christmas and New Year's. Living the expat life was like riding an emotional roller coaster. Being home was a huge high. It was exciting to spend time with close friends and family for days on end, like one continuous party—and then we flew back to Thailand. Inevitably, the high was followed by a huge letdown. I felt like an inflated balloon on the return flight, filled with delight in the beginning, then leaking out air slowly, until I was completely deflated by the time we landed in Bangkok. After we made our way through customs, we exited into the main corridor of the noisy airport. Once outside, we caught a taxi and stuffed our luggage into the trunk. Exhausted and tired, no one said much on the ride back to Nichada.

We returned the first week of January 2007, in time for Kris to start school. On our first morning back, I woke feeling listless with that familiar refrain in my head: *What will I do today?* I was awake but not ready to get out of bed. I stared at the clock, which read six. Muslim chants floated over the fence, my signal to get up and make coffee. I sat up and fumbled into my robe and flip-flops. I walked downstairs to the kitchen and measured the right amount of coffee into the grinder. The rich aroma of the beans smelled heavenly. I flipped on the electric coffee maker and headed for the living room where I sat cross-legged on my yoga mat to meditate. Closing my eyes, I dipped into a deep well of silence which reassured me. It was like entering my own private world of thoughts and feelings that no one else had access to. I remained seated there for some time until I heard Randall's footsteps like low drumbeats coming down the stairs.

Morning wasn't his best time. He often said he couldn't look at food until at least eleven. Leaning against the breakfast counter I asked, "What are your plans this week?"

"Work, and then I have a bike trip in Hua Hin this weekend. I'm hoping you can join me." He poured himself a cup of coffee, then looked up at me.

I was surprised by his request. I hadn't accompanied him on a bike expedition for at least six months. Our relationship was in flux in many ways. I'd become less emotionally dependent on him and no longer curbed my weekend activities to suit his schedule, even if it meant we spent less time together. Although we never formally talked about it, we'd reached a mutual understanding that our needs were different. While he pursued outdoor adventures, I spent more time at the temple.

But here I faced an uncomfortable dilemma. I paused to decide how I wanted to respond. I wondered why all of a sudden he wanted me to go with him. Maybe it had something to do with the fact that we had just had two weeks' vacation, and he wanted to spend more time together. I wasn't sure, but I wasn't riding a bicycle anymore, which meant going for the sake of keeping him company. I didn't really want to go, but I was hesitant to say no.

I thought about the last time I'd accompanied him. The ride took place over the weekend in a remote countryside location. We booked a motel room in advance since we knew we would be staying over Saturday night. I agreed to go, even though I knew I would probably be bored stuck in the middle of nowhere with nothing to do while Randall was off riding. It hadn't occurred to me to say no; I never wanted to disappoint him. I took a book to read and hoped to find a city nearby to explore as a distraction.

I recalled that we had driven about four hours south of Bangkok and then turned off the highway onto a dirt road. Handmade signs with arrows pointed us in the direction of the main entrance to the motel. *I'm in trouble,* I thought. There were no small towns nearby, and on first impression, the resort complex looked like an abandoned miniature golf course. We unpacked the car and checked into our room, which turned out to be the Thai equivalent of a cut-rate Motel Six. At $30 a night, there were no amenities—a sink, toilet, overhead fan, and two twin beds. I tried the main light switch, but it didn't work. "This room is dark and creepy," I said. Fortunately, the windows let in enough light to read by.

We walked back to the car, and Randall took his bike off the overhead roof rack. I noticed about forty people with bikes gathered near the front entrance, including several couples— all wearing cycling jerseys and cleats. For the next five hours, I would have to entertain myself until the riders returned.

It was blazing hot outside. I walked back to our room hoping to cool off and read my book, but I was too hot and sweaty to concentrate. I turned on the overhead fan since there was no air conditioning, and lay on the bed staring at the ceiling, feeling empty inside as if the life had drained out of me. I was completely uninspired. Had I been braver, I would never have agreed to come in the first place.

"Let me think about it," I said now, responding to Randall's request. My first instinct was, *Don't say anything, stall for time.* I knew I didn't want to go, but I didn't have the courage to say no. I struggled with stern voices in my head admonishing me, *You'd better not say no.* I couldn't identify the voices or where they were coming from, but they reminded me of a Greek chorus harping at me in the background. I spent the next few days mulling this situation over. How could one simple act of saying no to a weekend bike trip, one in which I wouldn't even be riding, become so huge in my mind? After much soul-searching, I realized that the voices were deep and ancient within me. These were the voices of my Jewish ancestors who demanded that I take care of my husband no matter the cost to myself, which meant silencing my own needs in an unspoken pledge not to disobey him. Nowhere is it written in the Jewish religion—or in any religion I'm aware of—that a wife should stay strong in her marriage and speak truth to power by saying no to her husband. I felt as if I were about to break an essential Old Testament covenant, an agreement buried deep in my bones telling me it was a sin to go against my husband's wishes. The guilt was overwhelming, like a weight pressing down on my shoulders.

I thought about my mother, a confusing role model for me as a child. She seemed both powerful and unhappy at the same time. Born to Orthodox Jewish parents who had emigrated from Russia in the early 1900s, my mother was the youngest of seven, the only child born in this country, and the first woman in her family to graduate from university. When I asked her to describe her mother, she would only say that she was forty-six, uneducated, and spoke only Yiddish in the home.

My mother, like many other women in the 1950s, became a housewife who simply grew disenchanted over time.

It's no wonder she seemed depressed. Her law degree sat on the shelf gathering dust as life passed her by. The mundane tasks of cooking and cleaning for others must have paled in comparison to her career aspirations to be a practicing attorney. When I was twenty-one, my mother, at age fifty-seven, tried to reinstate her law career. She took the California Bar three times, but failed to pass. After her third attempt, she was dejected. "I guess I've been out of school too long," she said. In that moment, all the resentment I had felt for my mother as a child evaporated into genuine compassion. It was one of the few times I felt close to my mother. She'd let her guard down, and her sudden honesty shocked me. I wanted to do something for her but felt helpless. All I could think to say was, "I still love you." Despite all the turmoil we'd faced, my mother was a strong woman who had sacrificed her dreams to serve her family, a mighty woman with a human heart after all.

I thought about Dhammananda, such a powerful role model for me. She had the courage to step out of the confines of her marriage, to free herself from the responsibilities for her husband and children, to embrace Buddhism. Not only did she have the courage to say no, she walked away from a thirty-year marriage.

My task seemed so simple compared to hers. I wasn't leaving my marriage; I was simply asserting my right to say no. I needed to overcome the powerful voices clamoring in my head, to disobey them, to find the courage to simply speak my truth.

Finally, on Thursday night, three days after his original invitation, I was ready to let Randall know I wasn't going, but I was nervous. My biggest fear was disappointing him, or worse, that he would start yelling at me. Before he turned on the TV, I said, "I need to talk to you."

"Okay," he said, a tinge of worry on his brow. "Is something wrong?"

"I thought about going with you this weekend, but I'd rather not," I said. "There's nothing for me to do while you're out riding all day, and I would feel lonely all by myself."

He grew quiet and didn't say anything. I guessed he was disappointed because all he did was turn on the TV. We didn't talk for the rest of the evening. It was an uneasy silence. Before going upstairs I asked him, "Are you mad at me?"

"You always ask me that," he said, exasperated. "I'm not mad. Just wish you were coming, that's all."

"I understand." I nodded, relieved.

I headed up to bed. As I brushed my teeth, it occurred to me that, even though I had feared the worst, a plague of locusts hadn't rained down on my head. I had taken a first step in the right direction. I was learning how to say no, growing stronger, and I felt proud of myself for asserting my own needs and speaking up for myself.

Saturday morning, after Randall left for the bike trip, I started writing my article on Dhammananda. I worked all weekend, and by Sunday evening I had a pretty good first draft to submit to the editor. I was delighted, but also worried. The project had been a major focus of my life for the past year. Now that it was nearing completion, once again, I would have big chunks of free time. Even though I planned to visit Dhammananda on weekends, I still needed something more to occupy my weekdays.

A few weeks earlier, my good friend Nancy had moved to downtown Bangkok, and with that our daily walks had stopped, though we continued to talk by phone. Still, we saw each other less frequently. I thought about finding meaningful volunteer work. Now would be the perfect time to start looking. I had recovered from surgery, and Kris was settled in school, so I spent the next few weeks researching volunteer opportunities. I loved being around children. A lot of women volunteered in the Thai orphanages, but taking care of small babies didn't appeal to me. I actually had some teaching experience in my early twenties when I was a teacher's aide in a third-grade public school classroom helping Spanish-speaking migrant children. With that experience in mind, I decided to see what volunteer opportunities there might be to work with school-aged kids.

The following day, the opportunity I was looking for seemed to fall out of the sky. Browsing through the ISB newsletter, I found an article about a project to raise funds for victims of the December 26, 2004, tsunami called the Tsunami Relief Network. In the immediate aftermath of the disaster, ISB had launched a fundraising campaign to help support a new school being built in Khao Lak, a popular beach resort near the site where a Dutch teacher from ISB had tragically lost his twin boys. The new school was called The 35th Rajaprajanugroh School (R35), and was a program of His Majesty the King's Foundation. R35 was being constructed to provide housing and education for tsunami orphans. It was exactly what I'd been looking for; my heart went out to these kids who had lost so much.

I contacted a member of the Executive Planning Committee and explained that I had previously worked as a fundraiser in my last job. The committee was eager to have me and invited me to attend their next meeting.

Within the first two weeks of joining the committee, I discovered the network was sponsoring a two-day event called Friendship Weekend. Once a year, ISB middle and high school students traveled down to R35 to spend a weekend with elementary school kids. The intent of the program was to encourage bonds of friendship between the two groups. Friendship Weekend would give me a chance to engage with young children, something I looked forward to. They needed eight parent volunteers to accompany the ISB students. My position on the Executive Planning Committee meant I could participate, and I signed up to attend the second weekend in March.

I decided to ask Kris to volunteer with me. Kris had a way with little ones, and I thought it might be a positive experience for him and for the kids. Wanting him to volunteer was partly selfish on my part; it would give me an excuse to spend time with him. Now that he was in high school, I saw him less often. Most weekends, he headed off to Bangkok in a taxi with his friends to movies, shopping malls, and occasionally paintball. I only had two weeks to convince him to come, which wouldn't be easy because I knew he would rather spend time in Bangkok with his friends. But I had a bargaining chip on my side. ISB had a community volunteer requirement that each student complete twenty hours of service. If Kris were to participate, he would fulfill the entire service requirement. I approached him after dinner. It was a delicious meal Durga had prepared of roti, samosas, and vegetable curry with rice.

As we finished eating, I posed the question: "Let me ask you something. How would you like to complete all of your community service hours in one weekend?"

Kris looked up at me suspiciously. "What's the catch, Mom?"

"Nothing," I said. "You have to complete twenty hours in the next three months, and this would be a way to do it."

"What do I have to do?"

"You'd travel with a group of twenty-five middle and high school students to Khao Lak for the weekend. You'd get to play games with elementary school kids. They're all disadvantaged kids and some are orphans who lost their parents in the tsunami."

"I'll do my volunteer hours, Mom. You're always worrying about me getting things done." This was his way of putting off something he had no interest in doing. Like any other fifteen-year-old boy, he wasn't thinking ahead. The conversation stalled for a minute until I thought of one more possible way to get him to participate.

"How about if we can convince Adam to come along?" Adam was Kris' best friend. Kris didn't respond immediately, which I took as a good sign. Maybe he was thinking it over.

"Let me talk to his mom," I said. "I'll let you know what she says."

Adam's mom was happy to let her son participate, and like me, she figured it hinged on both boys deciding they wanted to do it together. I was thrilled when they said yes, and my hopes for the weekend skyrocketed. I imagined Kris laughing and playing with the children. One or two kids would be hanging off him, unable to let go. By the end of the weekend, he would be sad to say goodbye. When we got back home I would ask him what he thought about the experience and he would reply, "I get it Mom, it's all about caring for others. I loved it when the little kids hugged me; I felt so special. I'll always remember this weekend. So glad you asked me to come." I had pretty lofty expectations of a fifteen-year-old.

The second weekend in March, Kris, Adam, and I joined twenty-five ISB students and eight parents late Friday afternoon to board a bus headed for the airport. The trip organizers had arranged for the parents to pay for the students to fly down to Khao Lak, since it would have been a ten-hour bus ride from Bangkok. Most of the ISB student volunteers were Thai. There were only a handful of non-Thai students, Kris and Adam among them. I hoped the language barrier wouldn't prevent Kris and Adam from interacting with the R35 kids.

We landed in a small airport in southern Thailand in the seaside town of Krabi, where we were picked up by buses. It was about a two-hour drive to the school and still daylight when we arrived. Along the way we passed stunning views of lush jungle landscape dotted with palm trees and mangrove forests. Towering limestone cliffs bordered the coastline with rocks jutting up from the sea. When we pulled into the gravelly driveway of R35, the kids ran up to greet us with big smiles. They were all ages, older and younger students. The ISB kids exited the bus with small tents and sleeping bags in tow. The Thai kids from ISB immediately started talking and interacting with the R35 students. I watched Kris and Adam straggle off the bus and shove into one another, stumbling and laughing. They didn't seem to pay much attention to the R35 kids, but I figured once the activities started they would get more involved.

Khun Luk, an R35 teacher with short clipped black hair, walked up to greet us. She spoke English and told us she would be our guide for the weekend. She directed our group to join her and then led the ISB kids to a small patch of grass to set up their tents. After getting the kids settled, she led the parents to our dorm rooms. She told us that a dinner bell would sound soon and that we should meet her downstairs.

As soon as the bell rang, Khun Luk was waiting for us. The Thai students from R35, all different ages and heights, waited for us outside. The older students, clearly from the upper grades, accompanied the younger ones, holding their hands as they made their way down a dirt path, apparently in the direction of the dining hall.

Next, Khun Luk led us to a grassy area to join the kids from ISB. We all walked together toward the dining area, a long open rectangular space with a concrete floor, wooden picnic tables and chairs, and a roof for shelter from the rain.

First, the R35 students lined up in an orderly fashion, waiting patiently to get their food. There must have been close to two hundred students. The older kids stood behind the younger children in line, hands on their shoulders, gently guiding them forward. Two younger boys, who couldn't have been older than ten, wobbled past us toting a large plastic tub of rice. It was clearly heavy because it took both boys, each with a firm grip on the handle, to deliver it. Dinner was served buffet style. The children knew when it was their turn, and one by one stepped up to get their food. The women servers ladled out large portions of rice, chicken, and vegetables to fill their plates. The food was hot and plentiful. When all the children were seated, it was our turn to be served.

I watched Kris and Adam out of the corner of my eye. They seemed more interested in eating than interacting with others. Kris could converse in Thai, so I hoped he would start talking to the R35 kids after dinner. I soon became engrossed in the conversation at my own table with the other parents, and by the time I looked up again, Kris and Adam were gone. After dinner Khun Luk and the other teachers called the kids together for relay races, and everyone joined in. There was lots of shouting, laughing, and encouragement from teammates as the runners ran as fast as they could up and down a grassy court to tag the next person in line. Around nine o'clock, the R35 kids headed back to their rooms and the ISB kids returned to their tents for the night. I saw Kris and Adam slip into their tents before I had a chance to say goodnight.

After breakfast the next morning, Khun Luk directed our group to a large open-air patio. About one hundred R35 students, ranging in age from eight to thirteen, sat cross-legged on the concrete floor waiting quietly for us. But the quiet soon exploded into peals of laughter, giggling, and shouting as the games got underway.

The teachers split the students into three different groups for activities. The first group played Bingo, the second group played musical chairs, and the third group made friendship bracelets. I stayed with the Bingo group while Adam and Kris headed off to play musical chairs.

A teacher handed out Bingo cards to the first group and asked, "Are you ready?" The students shouted in unison "Yes!" Curtis, an eighth-grader from our group with a mischievous grin, picked a number from the shoebox and waved it back and forth. Leaning in to get a closer look, another student called out, "Thirteen," as the R35 students stared down intently at their cards. After a series of numbers were called out a voice cried out, "Bingo!" A young Thai girl with short black hair who looked to be about eight ran up to the front eager to claim her prize. Her face lit up when Curtis handed her a white Teddy bear, which she clutched close to her chest.

Next our group rotated to the far end of the patio where the kids were making friendship bracelets, weaving beads onto colored strands of plastic. Phantila, a high school student from ISB, was surprised when her younger companion handed her a keychain. "It was very carefully made, and I could tell that she really liked it, but she insisted I have it anyway."

Although I was curious to know how Kris was doing, I decided to stop worrying about him and focus on myself. I was enjoying the kids, and they seemed to appreciate all the attention from the visiting students and parents. After lunch there was a game of tug-of-war and more relay races followed by ice cream. In late afternoon, it was time for us to head back. Saying goodbye wasn't so easy. Students lingered in small groups, arms wrapped around each other's shoulders, smiling for one last photo. They tore small scraps of paper and hastily exchanged phone numbers

On the bus ride back to the airport a high school student paused to reflect. "You feel so good; the kids' eyes light up when they see you. Just a little smile makes them really happy."

Another student said, "I like to think the kids will always remember me, because I will always remember them."

I sat back in my seat, and thought about everything that had happened in the past twenty-four hours. It was an intense weekend, and I was tired. Tears welled up as I flashed back to how kind the R35 kids had been with each other. There was a unity that came out of their suffering—ties of love and friendship that bound them together like one huge, close-knit family. They cared and looked after one another as if they were siblings. They'd lost so much, yet seemed happy. I knew there was more to their stories involving grief and loss, but I was not privy to those stories. Occasionally Khun Luk would allude to the fact that the kids were suffering from post-traumatic stress, but she never went into details about the particulars of their lives. The friendship exchange was intended to be a diversion for the R35 students, a chance for them to have fun, and they had seemed to enjoy themselves.

It was a humbling lesson for me to see how resilient the R35 students were in the face of their losses. I was also impressed that they responded so well to the simple attention and caring from the ISB kids. I was full of gratitude for these children and for the chance to be part of their lives.

When we landed in Bangkok, Kris and I gathered our suitcases at the airport, said our goodbyes, and headed out to find our driver. We didn't say much on the ride home. Kris seemed quiet and contemplative. I imagined he must have been silently absorbing the experience. I didn't ask him what he was thinking, since I didn't want to disturb him.

A few days later I asked Kris what he thought about the experience. He said, "It was okay. There was a really cute girl from my class that we talked to." My heart sank. What had I been thinking? Of course, he was just like any other fifteen-year-old, and his biggest focus was the things that mattered to him. I'd wanted Kris to have a life-changing experience, but Kris was just being himself, not the precious version I had concocted in my head.

On a personal level, I realized that regardless of Kris' experience, I'd had a wonderful time. My orientation to Kris was changing. As his mother, I would always be concerned for my son's wellbeing, but it was also okay for me to focus on my own needs and interests. My experiences were for me, and I no longer needed everything to hinge on whether or not Kris had a good time. This was new territory for me, a complete about-face. Instead of wondering how I could take care of others, I began to ask myself, *What do I want?* This wasn't easy for me, especially since I had learned as a child not to focus on myself or express what I needed.

Just as with Kris, my orientation to Randall was changing. Saying no to my husband was a big deal for me. As a young girl, I had learned to disguise my true feelings under a cloak of shame, and remained hidden to protect myself. Whenever I did summon up the courage to say no to my mother, she would get angry and send me to my room or tell me I was being selfish. I always felt like I had done something wrong or there was something wrong with me. For the first time, I was peeking out from underneath my cloak of shame and expressing my true feelings. Like a seed germinating in the rich, black soil, I had remained hidden until now, a plant in embryo form. With time, patience, and practice, I would eventually sprout into a seedling and transform into an adult plant with roots of my own.

Chapter 11:

Medicine Buddha Celebration

In early 2008, the construction of the Medicine Buddha Vihara was nearing completion, and Dhammananda began planning a special ceremony to unveil the Medicine Buddha. She chose April 6 for the unveiling because it marked the centenary of the birth of her mother, Venerable Maha Bodhi Dharmacaraya (Voramai Kabilsingh). If her mother had still been alive, she would have been one hundred years old that day. Dhammananda was very excited about the celebration and talked about it for months ahead of time. She wanted me to be there, and of course I wouldn't have missed it. I couldn't wait to see the Medicine Buddha uncovered again.

The night before the event, I was unable to sleep and woke early. While it was still dark outside, I crept around the bedroom, not wanting to wake Randall, got dressed, and went downstairs. I cracked open the front door and saw the driver waiting for me. I skipped my morning coffee, grabbed my water bottle, and climbed into the back seat of the car.

The headlights peered through the darkness, radiating a soft white light that illuminated the night sky.

On the drive down to the temple, I thought about my serendipitous first encounter with the Medicine Buddha. It had been two and a half years since I'd first wandered into the back garden and seen the Medicine Buddha uncovered. Every time I visited the temple, I hoped to see the Buddha again but never did. In the two years it took for me to fully recover from back surgery, I prayed every day to the Buddha asking for healing, and my prayers had been answered. I no longer suffered back pain and was able to return to all my former activities, including swimming, hiking, and skiing. I was convinced that the Medicine Buddha's healing radiance had helped me recover from my debilitating back injury. I wanted to kneel before the Buddha and express my gratitude. I could hardly contain my excitement to see the Medicine Buddha again.

We arrived at the temple before dawn on a misty, drizzly Sunday morning. The front gate was still locked. Our car's headlights lit up the entranceway and soon caught the attention of one of the nuns, who opened the gate. I was glad to arrive while the temple was still quiet and peaceful. It was early enough that the gong for morning chanting hadn't rung yet. As soon as it rang, I climbed the stairs to join the nuns on the second floor of the prayer hall.

After the chanting was complete, in keeping with the Sunday tradition, we went on alms round. We were walking down a side street, and the sky lit up pinkish orange as the sun rose over the horizon. We approached the first family, a grandmother, her daughter, and her granddaughter waiting for us. The grandmother's face looked familiar. She solemnly scooped rice from a large silver pot and ladled a spoonful into Dhammananda's alms bowl. Then her daughter handed Dhammavanna a small bunch of purple orchids. I stepped up just in time as Dhammavanna turned and handed the orchids to me, and I added them to the cart. We continued down the street and collected packets of curried vegetables, bunches of bananas, bottled water, flowers, and tropical fruits like mangosteen—a small purple fruit that looks like a tiny eggplant and tastes sweet with a slight tartness.

We returned with two full carts of food and ate a hearty breakfast. I always felt humbled by the local people who gave so much. I wondered if I would be able to give so generously living in such difficult circumstances. I donated money to the temple, but I could afford to. This felt different. People were getting up before dawn and preparing freshly cooked food. They opened their hearts and gave generously. I admired their commitment and learned from their example.

After breakfast, temple volunteers rushed around making last-minute arrangements for the festivities. I walked to the back garden and surveyed the vihara. The open stage that once housed the Buddha had been replaced by a tall white building with four wing-like alcoves attached to the center. The roof of the vihara had upturned eaves on the corners that were decorated with gleaming golden lotus blossoms pointing skyward as if in supplication. A set of stairs led up to the main shrine.

I climbed to the top of the stairs. The long wooden doors stood open revealing the Medicine Buddha inside. Two garlands of orange marigolds hung from atop the doorway, tied together at the bottom with a blue ribbon to be cut at the appropriate time. I was surprised when I looked through the open doorway and saw the outline of the statue uncovered. *How odd,* I thought, *to call it an unveiling ceremony even though the statue was completely visible.* Having waited so long to see the Buddha again, I had the sudden urge to venture inside to take a closer look, but I held back, afraid that I might be breaking a sacred tradition by looking at the Medicine Buddha ahead of the ceremony. I turned and wandered back to the main prayer hall.

By now, mid-morning, the sun was strong. Maejis, bhik-khunis, honored guests, and temple devotees mingled quietly near the temple entrance. I estimated there was a crowd of three hundred people there.

Suddenly, a loud crack broke the silence. Firecrackers strung on a nearby tree exploded, catching people by surprise and sending an electric surge of excitement through the crowd. A man chanted in low, deep tones, *"Buddham saranam gacchami"* (I take refuge in the Buddha). His voice boomed from a loud speaker in pounding beats that shook the ground underfoot.

As the smoke cleared, three young men dressed in shiny orange silk tops, green wrap-around pants, and broad white headbands stepped to the front of the line. They struck *kangsadarn* (flat brass bells) with wooden sticks—*thong, thong, thong.* Taking slow, deliberate steps, they led the procession forward. In the second row, Senator Watthana, a strong supporter of Dhammananda, carried the Thai flag, and beside her an elderly woman held the personal flag of H.M. King Bhumipol Adulyadej (Rama IX). A third woman carried a Sri Lankan Buddhist flag.

Next in line, four Thai men carried a pedestal draped in shiny gold satin and adorned with purple orchids. Seated in the middle of the pedestal was a miniature statue of the Medicine Buddha made of bronze, about eight inches high and five inches wide. A woman cradled a *sappathon* (large ceremonial umbrella) to shade the Buddha. Temple devotees followed in succession carrying baskets of flowers and Tibetan sticks of yarn that looked like the Mexican God's eyes I'd seen in Guadalajara. Caught up in what felt like a mystical procession, I joined the back of the line.

The procession made its way past the temple buildings and crossed the bridge into the back garden. When we reached the Medicine Buddha Vihara, I saw Venerable Dhammananda seated at the top of the stairs at the opening to the inner shrine. At her side was her teacher from Sri Lanka, Bhikkhuni Rahatungoda Saddha Sumana, waving a straw fan. A group of ten nuns dressed in saffron robes sat behind Dhammananda on the upper steps. I only recognized two of those nuns from the temple; the rest appeared to be from Sri Lanka.

Music began to play, and a group of four elegantly dressed Thai dancers outfitted in traditional silk costumes began to dance at the base of the vihara. They moved like devas surrounded by a sea of bubbles and white steam that floated skyward. It was as if they were dancing in clouds. One male dancer dressed in exquisite white satin and wearing an elaborate gold headpiece stepped forward. His face was angelic. Watching him, I felt as light as a feather, as if I were being lifted into the arms of an angel—suspended in a heavenly light. My body was tingling all over. His dance seemed to be an invitation from the gods welcoming everyone into a sacred realm. The dancers tossed flower petals and one-baht coins wrapped in red, blue, and orange tissue paper into the crowd. People scrambled in all directions scooping them off the ground. I felt a rising sense of excitement as the ceremony began.

After the dancers finished, Dhammananda rose to speak. She spoke in Thai, and I assumed she was welcoming the guests. After a few opening remarks, her face grew pensive and tears ran down her cheeks. Chills swept over me. I had never seen her so emotional before. I imagined this had to be quite an eventful day for her, and I looked forward to having her describe her feelings to me afterwards when we had a chance to talk.

After her speech, she and her preceptor cut the long garland of orange flowers that draped the entranceway, walked into the inner shrine, and sat in chairs to the right of the Medicine Buddha. The other nuns filed into a row of chairs behind her. A group of male monks entered the vihara and knelt on mats in the center of the room facing the Medicine Buddha. White plastic chairs were arranged to the left of the monks for laypeople. I was among a lucky group of about forty people who sat inside the vihara. The other guests sat outside in chairs arranged around the base of the vihara.

One of the Thai men who carried the miniature Buddha on the pedestal stepped forward and placed the small figure at the base of the larger, majestic blue Buddha. A maeji stepped up to the front with a long spool of *sai sin* (white string). She wrapped the twine around the smallest finger of the large Buddha's right hand and the thumb of his left hand that held the medicine bowl. Then she unwrapped more string, tied it around the smaller Medicine Buddha, and handed the free end to Dhammananda, who wound the string around her prayer book and passed it on to her preceptor. This continued with each nun wrapping the string around her prayer book so that everyone was connected to the healing essence of the Medicine Buddha.

Dhammananda began chanting and the nuns recited along with her. The chanting was broadcast on a speaker so that guests sitting outside could hear. I closed my eyes. The women's voices were light and airy like soft bells. My mind drifted in the sound. When the nuns finished chanting, the monks began. In contrast to the women, the male voices echoed in low, rich tones filling the inner sanctum of the vihara. The sound reverberated up and down my spine like steady drum beats. After the monks finished chanting, Dhammananda spoke first in Thai and then English. She thanked everyone for coming and let people know that the ceremony was over.

An electric surge of excitement lingered in the air. I was elated. I'd waited so long to see the Medicine Buddha uncovered, and now I couldn't contain my joy. It was as if a geyser had exploded through every pore of my body, shot up through the top of my head, and lifted my spirit up to the heavens—a huge opening. My heart expanded to encompass the love and gratitude I felt. While others left the vihara, I remained seated. I wanted to kneel before the Buddha and say a personal prayer of thanks, but there were still too many people around. I closed my eyes and prayed: "Oh, Blue Healer, thank you. You held me in the palm of your loving embrace, gave me my life back, and opened my heart so that I may see. I am forever grateful. May your divine light always shine upon me."

I pressed my palms together and bowed my head low. "Thank you, Wise Healer." I took a deep breath and slowly opened my eyes.

I felt profoundly peaceful, as though I'd crossed over a threshold into a new way of being. Just like the Medicine Buddha, until now, my essential self had lain veiled beneath my prescribed roles as wife and mother. No longer tethered to my husband's wishes nor bound by unrealistic expectations of my son, I felt as though someone handed me a key to a door. Now that the door had opened, I'd stepped into an exciting new world, free to say yes to myself and live life on my own terms.

As I left the vihara, I looked around. Everyone, including me, was smiling, our faces radiant. It was as if the Medicine Buddha held all of us in his divine embrace, uniting us into one beloved community.

Medicine Buddha

The crowd soon dispersed and headed back for lunch. I lingered for a few minutes in the garden and then walked back to the dining room. I had never seen so many people gathered there. Extra tables had been set up to accommodate the guests, and the room was full to capacity. I wanted to talk to Dhammananda, but there was a long receiving line, including married couples and families with elders and young children waiting to see her. As each group knelt before her,

Dhammananda recited a blessing. Even though I imagined she had probably been up since four o'clock, her face revealed no trace of exhaustion. *How does she do it?* I wondered. She looked so calm and focused on receiving one group after another. As the line died down I approached her table and knelt before her. She looked at me, her face filled with concern as if to say, *What do you need, how can I help you?* I asked if we could meet later to talk. She nodded and asked me to come by her office at two.

Just before two o'clock, I grabbed a cup of coffee. They had small packets of coffee labeled "Super Coffee 3-in-1"—an instant coffee blend of powdered milk, coffee, and sugar—that, under any other circumstance, I wouldn't have touched. But here at the temple, even instant coffee seemed like a delicacy. I poured the powder in my cup and added boiling water. Taking small sips, I walked to Dhammananda's office. The door was closed so I knocked quietly. She waved me in, her hand pointing to the chair on the opposite side of her desk. "Sit," she said, looking radiant. She had removed her outer robes and wore a simple shirt with pockets. "This is my traveling jacket," she said. She removed her glasses and set them on the desk.

"What would you like to talk about?"

"Do you remember what you were feeling in the beginning of the ceremony? I saw tears running down your cheeks."

Dhammananda looked off in the distance and said, "I felt my mother's presence. Everything was so beautiful I could hardly speak. There are only five of us living at our temple, and this ceremony was a huge undertaking. Everyone we asked was willing to lend a hand—lay members from my mother's time and people I had never met wanted to help. I was profoundly grateful to everyone for making this happen, and I felt all of us—participants, monks, and nuns—became one. The Medicine Buddha brought us together in a sacred connection."

"I felt that connection too," I said, honored that she was sharing such intimate feelings, especially the part about her mother. And yet I knew they'd had a challenging relationship. In a previous conversation, Dhammananda had told me how her mother sent her to live with her aunt in Bangkok to start her education when she was three and a half years old. Her mother was concerned about the quality of education in Trang, the southern province of Thailand where the family was living at the time.

Dhammananda talked about how lonely she'd felt when she was sent away. Her aunt didn't have any children of her own, and she never touched Dhammananda or held her. Dhammananda remembered coming home from preschool, and how she would wait outside her aunt's store and cry, craning her neck, looking up and down the street, waiting for her father to come get her. The workers making deliveries used to tease her and sang a Thai song: "Whose father is coming, whose tears are rolling down." Dhammananda said she suffered being cut off from her family in that way and felt a deep sense of loneliness that haunted her for years.

I asked if Dhammananda had ever been able to forgive her mother.

"It was a difficult relationship," Dhammananda said. "I was always expecting love but not getting it. Like on my birthday, I wanted a birthday cake. My mom said, 'That's sissy talk.' It wasn't until my mom was bedridden at age ninety-four that I realized she came from a family where she didn't have any love. I realized that my mother needed to be loved just like me. I felt so much compassion for her."

"Were you with her when she died?" I asked.

"No. I was in Paris, but I had a powerful experience the

night before she died. I felt heavy breathing in my left ear and woke up. That was my mother coming to say goodbye to me. The connection of our spirits was amazing."

I was struck by Dhammananda's love and compassion for her mother and how genuine it was, despite everything they'd been through. I longed to get to a place of such profound healing with my mother, to be able to love her despite my difficulties with her. I immediately understood that Dhammananda was more spiritually evolved than I was, but hoped that maybe I could get there—someday. Even though my mother and I had grown closer in her later years, I hadn't been able to forgive her for the way she'd treated me as a child. I still carried a grudge, a smoldering ember deep inside me that said she had been wrong to mistreat me.

For so long I had hung onto the belief that my mom was "the bad mother." If only she had been kinder and more nurturing toward me, I wouldn't have suffered so much. How could I ever forgive her for acting so cold, so mean, and so uncaring? Wasn't I the victim here? But now I realized something new—that if I forgave her, that would mean I could no longer blame her for feeling inadequate, for feeling less than and unworthy. Up until this very moment, I was convinced it was easier to blame my mother than to take responsibility for myself. My life had felt like a mess for so long, it never occurred to me that I could change things for the better.

Dhammananda exemplified a woman who was totally at peace with herself, vulnerable and forgiving of her mother who had hurt her so much. I longed to unlock what she had— some secret that would allow me to move from my stance of unrelenting blame to one of love, forgiveness, and acceptance. I suspected the missing ingredient for me was learning to take care of myself, love myself, and embrace myself just as I was, flaws and all. If I were honest with myself, I would have to take a leap of faith in order to accept and nurture myself, but I wasn't there yet.

As I bid farewell to Dhammananda she looked at me tenderly and reached out to hold my hand. It was such a loving gesture, as if she recognized something in me that I wasn't yet able to acknowledge in myself. My heart swelled with love. I looked into her soft brown eyes and whispered, "Thank you." She smiled and nodded silently. Perhaps this was what was meant by the term "heavenly grace" because I felt an inner light had been kindled. I bowed before her and slowly rose from my seat overwhelmed with gratitude as I walked out the door.

Outside the sun was beginning to set, and the sky was ablaze with a display of celestial colors—yellow, pink, and orange. I paused to soak in the sunset, as if to imprint the scene in my mind. I wanted to remember this day, all that it had encompassed. I'd arrived before it was light and was leaving now just as dusk was settling in, having undergone what felt like a profound change. I felt as though something had been unlocked deep inside me. I couldn't say exactly what it was, but I felt as if I had expanded into a fuller, more powerful sense of myself.

It was dusk by the time my driver passed through the temple gates to take me home. I settled in the back seat and stared out the window. My mind was clear of chatter, peaceful, and calm. I felt immersed in a cocoon of Dhammananda's love, which shielded and protected me from outside distractions. I likened where I was in my life to a caterpillar in the early stages of transformation. I understood what it felt like to be loved but wasn't sure I was capable of loving myself. I began to think about what it would mean if I were to begin to acknowledge myself. So many thoughts went through my head.

Just like women everywhere, I had been taught from an early age to take care of others. The thought of focusing on myself conjured up the word *selfish*. Why was it whenever I attempted to stand up for myself as a young girl, my mother called me selfish? I also experienced that in my marriage. It seemed the times I tried to tend to my own needs, I felt guilty. A voice would pop into my head: *You don't really care about others, you just care about yourself.* I never used the word *selfish*, but the meaning was implied.

All through history, society has condoned the idea that it's not okay for women to take care of themselves. We are supposed to be the nurturers, the caretakers, the feeders of others. But who reminds us to feed ourselves? I recalled the feminist wave of the 1970s, when we staged a mini-revolution in the name of becoming ourselves, reaching our human potential as leaders, scientists, politicians, artists, teachers, and spiritual leaders. I realized how much of myself I'd been giving away. I'd been doing it my whole life, unconsciously, but also at a cost. As the old saying goes, "We can't truly love another until we first love ourselves." I could see it was time for me to begin to practice; otherwise, I might never be free from the maternal wounds that bound me.

When we pulled up to the house, I experienced a Queen Esther moment. I opened the front door and felt a sense of pride in myself, that warm flash of recognition that I mattered, that I was loved, that I was okay just as I was. This was a small step forward for me, but it was also huge. Like a marathon runner who has run a good race, I felt as though I could make it to the finish line.

Chapter 12:

Sliding into Grace

We moved back to the States in June of 2008. In the mornings I would wake up feeling lost and confused. I would stand and stare out the front kitchen window, untethered from my new life. I missed Durga. Without her help, I easily fell back into my old role, taking care of the family, cooking dinner, and managing the household. I also missed Dhammananda. Without her spiritual guidance, I reverted to old behaviors, neglecting myself and serving others. It's not surprising that since we'd returned from Thailand, I'd grown depressed and withdrawn. I felt confined by my new lifestyle and yearned to be back in Thailand.

I often thought back to the last three months in Thailand, a high point in my spiritual development. I had rejoiced in seeing the Medicine Buddha unveiled. That ceremony marked my transition into a new phase of learning to love and accept myself. But all that progress faded when we left Thailand. On my own, without Dhammananda's love and guidance, I lacked the internal scaffolding to sustain my own emotional and spiritual growth.

As the years passed, I maintained email contact with Dhammananda. She encouraged me to try to find a spiritual teacher at home, but I never found anyone I could trust the way I trusted her.

It took six years, but finally I realized I had to go back. I needed to see Dhammananda again, to sit in her presence. I hoped that by spending time with her, I would come into contact with that essential part of myself that I'd felt so strongly in Thailand and that had gone missing.

I planned my trip for January of 2014, six and a half years after we'd left. I decided to stay at the monastery for four days and then visit Nancy in Bangkok at her apartment for a week. Boarding a plane at midnight, I landed in Hong Kong fourteen hours later. I didn't sleep at all and was exhausted by the time I got there. Fortified by a cup of coffee, I began to wake up. Somewhere between Hong Kong and Bangkok, the reality of what I was doing began to sink in: *I am going to see my teacher, Venerable Dhammananda.* Relief washed over me. I had twelve thousand miles behind me and was confident that I had made the right decision. When I disembarked from the plane in Bangkok, I found a taxi, pulled out my map to the temple written in Thai for the driver, and headed straight for the temple.

Drowsy in the back seat of the taxi, I suddenly snapped awake once we got to the main highway of Nakon Pathom. Noisy trucks and cars lined the busy street. It was easy to miss the temple, so I focused my attention, looking for the shining Chinese Buddha at the entrance to Songdhammakalyani Temple.

"*Leo sai*" (turn left), I exclaimed in Thai to the cab driver. He swerved, making a quick left turn into the main entrance. Within minutes, I saw the enormity of the changes that had taken place at the temple since I'd last been there. Behind the dining area was a formidable three-story concrete skeleton of a building. I had heard Dhammananda was planning to build a new international study center for ordained Theravada Buddhist women from Thailand, Sri Lanka, Indonesia, and Vietnam, but I had no idea that construction had already begun.

Dragging my luggage, I made my way down the gravel path to the front office. Dhammavanna was inside. When she saw me she stood up to greet me. "You come to see us again." She gave a tentative half-smile as if to say, glad to see you, but in a somewhat formal manner. I'm sure she had seen many visitors come and go since my last visit. I wanted to blurt out how much I had missed her but thought better of it. It would take time for her to warm to me again. "You come from the airport?"

"Yes, just now."

"You must rest. I take you to your room."

She grabbed a key and walked me down the central path. "This is the new library," she said, pointing with pride to a one-story building on the right. "Our old library was flooded, and we had to build a new one." She continued down the path to a three-story building with doors that were numbered on the outside.

"This is our new dormitory," she said. Dhammavanna led me up a set of stairs to the second floor where she unlocked a door to a private room marked 22. I was shocked when I surveyed the room. The wooden chaise lounges were gone, replaced by two twin beds with thin, two-inch mattresses on top. In the past I'd slept on a hard wooden surface. It would be such a blessing to have a real bed! The bathroom looked pretty much the same: a toilet, sink, and a large twenty-gallon trash can filled with water that served as the shower. I remembered how in the past I had taken cold showers, scooping out the cold water with a plastic bucket and dousing myself. I was so hot and sweaty from the flight that the thought of dumping cold water over me sounded refreshing. After Dhammavanna left, I removed my clothing and took a quick shower. I put on clean clothes and looked around. *Now what do I do?* I glanced at my watch. It was three o'clock. At four we would start work in the garden. In my free hour I decided to walk back to the Medicine Buddha Vihara and spend some time meditating there.

As soon as I left the room and closed the door behind me, I saw Dhammananda walking toward me from the far end of the walkway.

Nervous, I stumbled slightly. I had rehearsed this moment so many times in my head, and now that it was here, I felt awkward. I knelt down at her feet and bowed three times to show her the proper respect.

"You look so good," she said, greeting me warmly. She grasped my hands as I stood up, my face flushed with excitement. I was so happy to see her again. Slowly it dawned on me: *I'm here with my teacher.* She had the same peaceful expression I always remembered. I breathed a sigh of relief.

Her eyes lit up. "I have so much to tell you," she said, "but right now I have a guest to receive. You take a rest and we will talk later."

She whisked past me, and I watched her disappear down the stairwell at the other end of the walkway.

My heart sank for an instant. I had traveled all this way and anticipated this moment for so long. I sighed with disappointment. I wanted to sit with her one-on-one and talk, but I would have to be patient and wait a little longer, which wasn't easy for me. I paused for a moment to collect myself.

I wondered what Dhammananda had been doing up here on the second-floor walkway of the dormitory. I walked to the end and discovered a little office there with a desk and computer. It occurred to me that this must be Dhammananda's new office space. I turned and headed back in the opposite direction and climbed down the stairs.

I made my way to the Medicine Buddha Vihara in the back garden. Inside it was completely silent. I removed my shoes and felt the cool marble floor against my hot bare feet. Seeing the majestic blue Buddha brought tears to my eyes. I remembered how I had felt six years before, how elated I was at the unveiling ceremony. I dropped to my knees, bowed my head three times, and said a prayer as warm tears slid down my cheeks.

"Thank you, Blue Healer. I am asking for your help. I have lost my way. Please lead me out of the darkness into the light." I rose to my feet and stopped to admire the gleaming blue color of the Medicine Buddha. I decided to do a walking meditation. Moving in slow motion I inhaled and lifted my right foot a few inches off the floor. Stepping down on my right foot I exhaled and whispered, "Heel, toe." Inhaling again, I raised my left foot. As I placed my foot down I exhaled and repeated these words, "Held in the palm of the Buddha." I continued to move forward at a snail's pace, repeating the mantra over and over again. I got so absorbed in what I was doing that I lost track of time. When I looked at my watch it was almost four o'clock. I bowed before the beautiful blue healer and left feeling peaceful and content.

I walked back to the front office and found Dhamma-vanna, who told me to wait outside, and we would gather soon to rake leaves in the garden. All of a sudden the jet lag snuck up on me. All I wanted was to shut my eyes and lie down. I asked Dhammavanna if I could head back to my room to rest instead of joining everyone in the garden, and she nodded a silent permission to go.

I probably didn't need to ask, but it felt important to me. There were certain unspoken expectations, and I wanted

Dhammavanna to know that I took the commitment seriously and wouldn't skip out without a good reason.

Back in my room, I set my alarm for six thirty so I wouldn't miss the evening chanting. When the alarm rang, I woke in a daze. At first I didn't recognize where I was. I stared at the bare walls and summoned every ounce of energy I had to sit up. Then I forced myself to stand, shuffled toward the door, and slid on my flip-flops.

I was still groggy as I made my way into the main prayer hall. I counted twelve women in saffron robes lined up behind Dhammananda. Four were sameneris, novice nuns, dressed in brown robes, and eight were fully ordained bhikkhunis in saffron robes. Three women dressed in white, maejis, lined up behind the nuns and, following them, four young women dressed in T-shirts and jeans. Six years earlier when I'd last visited the temple, there were only two ordained women in addition to Dhammananda living there. I had expected there would be one or two more bhikkhunis at the temple, but there were eight. Dhammananda had made tremendous progress in achieving her dream of building a community of ordained women.

I scrambled into place at the end of the line as Dhammananda led the group forward up the steep narrow stairs to the second floor. I took a seat in the back of the room. In front of me the women knelt on floor mats.

As the chanting began, I took a deep breath and closed my eyes. The familiar refrains were music to my ears. After chanting we sat for twenty minutes and meditated. I fought to stay awake, nodding off and then catching my head as it dipped forward. *How embarrassing,* I thought. My first night and I was falling asleep. *What if someone sees me?* When the meditation finished, everyone quietly got up from their seats and walked downstairs. Normally I would have headed to the dining area to join the others for a cup of tea, but that night all I could think of was walking back to my room and falling into bed. I didn't even have the energy to get undressed. I lay down and shut my eyes. Next thing I knew, my alarm woke me at five o'clock in time to get ready for morning prayers.

I made my way to the main prayer hall in the dark with a small flashlight. After chanting and meditation, everyone walked downstairs to perform morning chores. Just like everyone else, I grabbed a broom to sweep the leaves off the concrete walkways that surrounded the prayer hall. It seemed there was never an idle moment, and the nuns were always working. In half an hour the gong rang for breakfast. I took a seat by a young Thai woman named Jieb whom I knew from previous visits to the temple.

Dhammananda once told me that Jieb had come to live at the temple when she was twelve. I didn't know why she came at such a young age but guessed her family couldn't take care of her. Dhammananda had supported her financially all through her school years up to receiving her BA degree. Now in her thirties, Jieb assisted Dhammananda in office matters and grew vegetables on raised beds in a beautiful garden outside the dining area. As soon as we finished eating, Jieb headed out to the garden. I watched her carefully tending the plants and watering them, lavishing her attention on them as if they were small children. I admired her dedication. Like so many women at the temple, she was committed to sustaining the well-being of the community. Even though Jieb spoke little English, I felt a special connection to her. She always brought platters of fruit for the whole table to share. Like so many of the women at the temple, she made me feel welcome.

I was just about to get up and leave when I caught a glimpse of Dhammananda headed in my direction.

"Did you sleep well?" she asked. I nodded and she handed me a piece of red fruit, with hairy tendrils. "Rambutan," she said smiling. "Taste it; it's so sweet. When you have finished, come see me in my office. It's at the end of the second floor of the new building." When she turned around to be on her way, I hurriedly washed my dishes. I couldn't wait to see her.

Dhammananda was busy working on her computer when I arrived less than ten minutes later, but when she saw me, she stopped and pointed to the chair opposite her.

The first thing I did was apologize for not coming to visit in such a long time, but she brushed aside my concerns.

"Have you found a teacher?" She looked intently into my eyes.

"No," I replied. "I've been to a Buddhist center many times, but I haven't found anyone who embodies the teachings like you." She nodded. I wanted to tell her how much I had missed her, to fill her in on everything that I'd been thinking about in recent years, about how unanchored I had been and how I longed to feel a spiritual connection again, but like so many times before when we met together, she led the conversation. She was excited about the new International Training Center under construction, her upcoming seventieth birthday, and her appointment as *pavattini* in November. I didn't know what pavattini meant so she explained it to me. She said that once a woman had been ordained for twelve years she was promoted to pavattini, meaning someone who could train novice nuns. In 2001, when Dhammananda was ordained as a sameneri, her teacher from Sri Lanka, Venerable Sumana, was her pavattini.

Dhammananda's face grew animated as she described the upcoming ceremony to celebrate all three events—completion of the new building, her birthday, and her appointment as pavattini. "On December 5, I will give temporary ordination to one hundred eight women," she told me. I'd never heard of temporary ordination. When I asked her about it, Dhammananda relaxed and settled back in her chair. She said it is typical for young men to take temporary ordination before they are married, like a rite of passage when they leave home for two to three months to live in the monastery as monks. She told me that in Thai culture, people believe children are indebted to their parents, especially their mothers who bring them into this world and raise them. Ordination is one way to "make merit," or repay this debt to their mothers.

"I want to give women the same opportunities as men," she said, sitting up and straightening her back. She felt it was important that women, especially professionals with a college degree, understood that women could be ordained just like men. In 2009, Dhammananda began to offer temporary ordination to women twice a year in April and December. She described the process. "They spend nine days at the temple. They take ten precepts, study the spiritual teachings of Buddhism, shave their heads, wear the robes, and practice meditation in hopes of improving their overall peace and contentment once they return to their normal lives." Her description reminded me of taking an experiential workshop, which in this case would involve enrolling in a course in monastic life, but just for a short time.

Listening to Dhammananda's soothing voice, I began to slow down and stop worrying about where the conversation was headed. I marveled at her ability to stay in the present. She talked to me as if we had just spoken yesterday and were continuing an ongoing conversation, as if no time had passed at all. I felt that one-on-one connection to her I'd missed for so long. This was the magic of our connection, that we could rekindle it at any moment. Our relationship endured, regardless of the time and distance that had separated us.

We had talked for about fifteen minutes when she reminded me that it was Saturday morning, the time to do sitting and walking meditation in the Medicine Buddha Vihara.

Although I wished we could talk longer, I felt the warmth of her caring and was satisfied. I tingled all over with happiness, a feeling that spread from my toes up through the top of my head. I felt my spirit begin to shine from within. I was back with my spiritual teacher, a wise woman who, like a mother bird, took me under her protective wing.

We walked together to the back garden. By the time we arrived, all the nuns and temple women were kneeling on mats facing the Medicine Buddha waiting for Dhammananda to arrive. Dhammananda took a chair in front to the right of the Medicine Buddha and held a microphone in her hand. She asked us to stand for walking meditation. She called me to the front and paired me up with one of the senior bhikkhunis. There was a serious tone in her voice. I knew from past experience that she felt I needed instruction in how to do walking meditation. I was nervous as I stepped to the front. I didn't like being watched too closely, as if I were being judged for my shortcomings. The nun looked at me with a bemused smile, but I was too self-conscious to relax and smile back.

I took my first step hesitantly with the nun alongside me. She must have sensed I was anxious because she immediately commented in broken English, "Walk like you in a garden. Think about present. Take time." She cocked her head slightly and looked at me. Perhaps she wondered if I was up to the task. With each breath I felt the solid sensation of the marble floor beneath my feet. We walked slowly and deliberately for twenty minutes. This single activity demanded my full concentration. My mind drifted back and forth. *Held in the palm of the Medicine Buddha,* I reminded myself. Still, I couldn't wait until the exercise was over, and I sighed with relief when Dhammananda rang the final gong.

"Now return to your places for guided meditation," Dhammananda said. I closed my eyes. Dhammananda spoke in low, soft tones. "Imagine taking a blue light into your heart," she said. I imagined the Medicine Buddha's blue healing light filtering through the top of my head into my heart. "Suffering and happiness come and go," she said. "The nature of suffering is always changing. You can always inhale healing blue energy and let it touch your heart. Then you exhale and send that positive energy outward to the people you love." I was deep into the meditation by now, inhaling a blue light and exhaling that blue healing energy to surround my husband and son. It was a powerful feeling. As the meditation drew to a close, I breathed deeply, completely calm and relaxed by this point. I walked silently from the vihara and returned to my room to rest and write in my journal until lunchtime.

At mid-afternoon, under the shade of a gazebo near the front office, I saw Dhammananda seated with three other nuns. As I came closer, she waved me over to sit down. She pulled out bags of moist clay and broke off a chunk for each person. She wanted us to make a family of clay birds. She dipped her hands in water and rolled the clay between her palms into the shape of a cylinder. Next, she broke off the top section and rolled it on the table. She seemed adept at shaping the clay into the head of a bird. She didn't talk much, but watched us as we attempted to work the clay with our fingers. I dipped my hands in water, rolled the clay between my palms, and began molding it into the shape of a bird's head and body with my fingertips. My bird's head was too thick and drooped over the body. "It's too heavy," I said, looking at the misshapen head.

"The clay is too wet," Dhammananda said. She picked up my bird and reshaped the head. Next, she added more clay to the body and built a solid base. Dhammananda gave a nodding look of approval as she handed the bird back to me. The bird looked much improved, and it stood without toppling over. I looked around the circle. Everyone's creation was unique. Dhammananda surveyed the family of birds. "Good," she said. This was an aspect of Dhammananda that I loved, her playful side.

In contrast, she could be stern at times. Once during morning prayers, she clapped her hands and stopped the nuns from chanting. She insisted that they repeat certain verses that she felt hadn't been recited correctly. I had also seen her reprimand the nuns when she grew impatient with them. She did not give up easily when she felt the women weren't performing to certain standards.

Although she had never reprimanded me, she had been quite serious with me earlier that morning when pairing me up with the experienced nun to do walking meditation. When she saw an opportunity for improvement, she provided the appropriate training. She took on many different roles at the temple: abbess, teacher, nurturer, and defender of her flock.

The next day, Sunday, the nuns did weekly alms round. Dhammananda no longer went on alms round; instead Dhammavanna led the procession of three nuns, two maejis, and me. There were also two young Thai women who walked alongside us pushing the cart to collect the food. Dhammavanna unlocked the front gate and stepped out into the cool morning darkness. We walked for a short block on Petkasem Highway as cars *wooshed* by us. Barking dogs trailed us, and I became nervous, afraid they might bite. The nuns just ignored them, and I tried to but was less successful. Eventually the dogs simply lost interest and retreated.

We turned off the main highway onto a quiet side street. A mother and daughter stood in front of a one-room storefront with a corrugated tin awning overhead. The little girl, who looked to be about four, stood barefoot next to her mother. As the nuns approached, the little girl stepped closer to her mother who bent down to her daughter's level, and encouraged her to scoop rice into Dhammavanna's wooden alms bowl. Then the mother and daughter knelt down and bowed their heads. The bhikkhunis chanted a prayer and gave them each a bottle of blessed water, turned, and made their way back down the side street.

Suddenly a young man came running after them with an aluminum bowl. When he caught up with the nuns, they slowly turned around to face him. He reached into his bowl, took a generous scoop of rice, held it to his forehead, said a brief prayer, and placed the rice into Dhammavanna's bowl. Then he knelt down. Seeing that man bow down before the nuns brought tears to my eyes.

I thought of Dhammananda and how, in an act of defiance, she had planted the seed for women to become ordained. Ten years ago, men had never even seen a female monk, much less bowed down in her presence. To watch this young man kneel before these women with such humility was very moving to me. He raised his palms to his forehead and earnestly whispered a prayer while the nuns recited their blessing. All eyes focused intently on this man as he continued to pray.

I hadn't been on alms round in many years, but I'd had an experience once or twice before that I call sliding into grace. It was like being drawn into a human circle of caring with no beginning and no end, like surrendering to that invisible cord of love that connects us all.

As alms round drew to a close and we headed back to the temple for breakfast, I thought about the experience. What made it so special? Perhaps we had witnessed a moment of human faith in all its reverence. Faith doesn't come easily to many of us, at least not to me, but we can create it through simple prayer. Our hopes, our dreams, and our despair all rest in the arms of our divine maker. I don't know what dreams this man held in his heart, but I'm convinced his prayers were heard that day.

After breakfast we did a special morning meditation in the Medicine Buddha Vihara. Dhammananda led another guided meditation on loving kindness. She encouraged us to imagine taking in ripples of yellow healing light into our hearts. Then she asked us to send that light outward to those we loved. Finally, she asked us to share our light with our adversaries. It was a beautiful meditation on the power of sharing compassion and loving kindness with ourselves and others.

The next day, Monday, was my last day at the temple. The time had gone by quickly, and I was sad to leave so soon. I couldn't imagine going home to the same dreary life I had been living. During my short stay here, my heart had opened. I'd reconnected to my spiritual self, a part of me that had lain dormant for the past several years. I was afraid I'd close down again once I got home. I had to find some way to sustain the momentum of what I had gained but knew it would be difficult without regular visits with Dhammananda.

After breakfast I approached Dhammananda at her table and knelt at her feet. I was leaving in about half an hour. I asked if I could talk with her for a short time in her office because I was having a hard time saying goodbye. Dhammananda nodded and told me to come see her in fifteen minutes.

As I approached her office door, my throat tightened. I walked in, and she motioned for me to sit down. Unable to prevent it, I started to cry. My voice cracked as I stumbled over my words. "I don't want to say goodbye. I don't want to go back home."

Dhammananda leaned toward me and kindly said, "I know transitions are hard for you. You might end up making a new connection. Who knows?" Then she laughed lightly. "Mission possible, not impossible."

I sniffled and wiped away my tears. "I have tried to meet other teachers, but you understand me in a way that no one else does."

"Take me with you," she said. "You don't have to lose me just because you are going away. Email me anytime you want. I correspond right away."

There was silence for a moment except for the birds chirping outside. I felt relief just talking to her. Dhammananda continued, "Nothing is permanent."

I nodded.

"Start looking at things in a new fashion. We never see things as they really are. Start to notice the beauty in little things. It's very refreshing. We always expect happiness in life. Sometimes happiness is the way you see things. There's always more than one way to look at things." I floated in our conversation, savoring her presence. I wanted to remember this moment when I got home. I knew there was little more I could say, so I tried to be brave. "I'll be back sooner the next time," I promised.

"Yes. Next time you come, the International Center will be finished." She smiled at me.

I sat there and etched her face in my mind, committing it to memory. "Thank you," I said and bowed. "I will email once I get home."

"Good, good," she replied.

I left the office and stepped out into the sunlight. Just as she suggested, I held her in my heart. "I'll come back,"

I whispered softly and touched my heart as I walked away. I grabbed my luggage from my room and headed back to the front office to wait for the taxi. I looked up at the large, Chinese Buddha and gave a wistful sigh. *I'm no good at saying goodbye.* Dhammananda was teaching me a new way of letting go.

As a child, I had thought goodbye meant permanently severing a relationship. Once I left, I feared I would never see the person again, and the connection would be broken forever. Now I had the opportunity to reinvest in our relationship over time, to learn that just because I wasn't with Dhammananda didn't mean we were lost to each other forever. Perhaps this was an instance of faith in the making. I needed to have faith that I could continue on my own and trust that I would see my teacher again. One thing was certain: I was committed to seeing Dhammananda again, so I would have plenty of time to practice letting go. I tucked her memory in my heart for safekeeping until we could be together again.

Chapter 13:

Ordained

O n the ride back to Bangkok, I shared the taxicab with a young Thai woman whom I'd seen at the temple dressed in white as a maeji. Now she had changed back to jeans and a T-shirt. We sat in the back seat and started up a conversation. "I'm going to Bangkok for two weeks," she told me. "When I come back I will be ordained as a sameneri and live at the temple with the other nuns." I thought about her, how hard it would be to live apart from family and friends, to give all that up for a life of devotion and service to others. I wondered what it would be like to commit to such an austere way of living. She would be making a long-term commitment to be ordained, not just temporary ordination. From now on, she would be dedicating her life to study the Dhamma and to serving others.

I admired her thick, shoulder-length, black hair and tried to imagine what she'd look like with her head shaved. I couldn't imagine her without hair. I was curious what it would feel like to shave my head. What would I look like with no hair?

I gazed out the window of the cab and thought about my recent conversation with Dhammananda. She was so excited about the upcoming December ordination. This was to be a temporary ordination. The women would make a two-week commitment to live at the temple, during which time they would shave their heads, wear the robes, and take ten precepts. I didn't know exactly what taking on ten precepts meant, but I figured they were similar to the Ten Commandments of Judaism.

Suddenly it dawned on me that I might come back in December and receive temporary ordination. I was missing Dhammananda, and I'd barely left the temple gates. I wanted to honor her on her seventieth birthday. I had some reservations about what it would be like to shave my head, but I reassured myself that my hair would always grow back.

I grew excited as I thought about how wonderful it would be to see Dhammananda again in December, and to show my devotion to her by being ordained. In that instant, sitting in the cab, everything came into focus: *I want to be ordained.* I knew how much it would mean to Dhammananda, and that meant a great deal to me.

I spent the next week in Bangkok with Nancy. We had a wonderful time together and, just like at the temple, my time there flew by. Soon after I returned home, I bought my ticket to Thailand. I decided to fly back in late November. In addition to buying a ticket, I looked on the temple's website (thaibhikkhunis.com) to find out how to register for the ordination ceremony. The first requirement was to write a 250-word essay answering the question, why do I want to be ordained? The second was to pay two hundred American dollars in fees. Though I wasn't necessarily interested in the religious commitment of becoming an ordained Buddhist for two weeks, it seemed like an opportunity to demonstrate my love and devotion to my teacher and to receive her spiritual blessing.

I knew my true motivation for going was to honor my teacher, but I wasn't sure I wanted to say that in my essay. I was afraid Dhammananda might only accept people who demonstrated a more serious commitment to studying Buddhism. But when I emailed Dhammananda to tell her that I wanted to take temporary ordination, she was supportive. She didn't ask me any questions, she simply reassured me by saying, "Don't bother writing the essay, just register so you will get the residential building rather than having to stay in a tent." I was relieved and sent off my registration fee right away. Over the next ten months my excitement grew, and by November I couldn't wait to see Dhammananda again.

The weekend after Thanksgiving, I flew back to Bangkok, grabbed a taxi, and headed directly to the temple. I arrived a few days early, hoping to get settled before everyone else arrived. When I stepped out of the taxi, Dot Com, the friendly white dog with the long, pointed nose and black spots, rushed up to greet me. Dhammavanna stepped out of the office and took me to the room that I would be sharing with two other women. It was a tiny space, but nothing could get in the way of my happiness.

Dhammavanna instructed me to pick up my clothing. She explained that for the first few days I would be wearing all white like a maeji, but after the ordination ceremony, I would dress in saffron robes. She walked me over to a small building I hadn't been in before. Inside there were two nuns busy working at sewing machines. Dhammavanna spoke to them in Thai. They walked over to a set of wooden shelves, pulled out all new clothing—a white top and a wraparound skirt still sealed in clear plastic—and handed it to me. I checked the size of the blouse. Whereas I was a size medium at home, there I was a size large. They rummaged through more shelves and brought me saffron robes, also brand new. The last thing they handed me was a brown top and wide leg pants, a set of work clothes for the garden. I went back to my room and changed into the white blouse and skirt. I looked at myself in the mirror and smiled. I was eager to get started, but it would be a few more days before the actual training process began.

That next morning after breakfast Dhammananda pulled me aside and asked for my wedding ring. She assured me that she would take good care of it and return it after the ceremony was over. I didn't question why she wanted my ring; I assumed it had something to do with one of the precepts, to remain celibate during the process of ordination. I twisted and turned the ring, struggling to get it off my finger. Having been married for twenty-eight years, I had rarely removed it except for an occasional cleaning. I felt naked without it but also lighter. Removing my ring gave me permission to leave everything behind. Here at the temple, I was no one's wife or mother. I was free to explore who I was on my own terms.

Over the next two days, women began arriving. I looked for other foreigners, but as it turned out I was the only farang among 124 Thai women. I was surprised because I assumed there would be other foreigners there. The following day rehearsals began. We each were given a white tag with a number on the front, like a nametag in a clear plastic cover with a pin on the back. My number was 122. We were asked to stand in a line in numerical order. Since I was 122, I was second to the last person in line. Every time an instruction was given, it was spoken in Thai. I felt like a child, dependent on my neighbors to guide me, but it was fun. People paid special attention to me because I was a foreigner. People cried out in English, "Khun Cindy, over here!" They would take my arm and lead me to where I was supposed to be. People treated me with kindness, like a sister they watched out for. I was touched by how well they took care of me.

The morning preceding our ordination, we prepared to have our heads shaved. I took my place near the end of the line, wearing my white top and skirt. Now that the moment had arrived, I felt removed from it all, as if I were a participant in a scene, watching from the sidelines. Part of me wanted to remain invisible so I wouldn't have to feel how nervous I was. It was a way to protect myself in a situation where I felt scared and out of control. I watched as devoted Thai family members began to arrive, mostly mothers and fathers. In keeping with tradition, they had come to honor their daughters. They were seated in chairs placed on either side of our procession. A beautiful Thai song played on the loudspeaker. I found out later it was a tender tribute to a mother's love.

Each young woman knelt before her parents, who handed her a large green leaf with two sticks of incense and a garland of flowers. I felt a tinge of sadness that my husband and son weren't there. Randall supported me and was proud of me for going. I tried not to think about it and to focus instead on what was happening around me.

I was paired with a Thai woman who looked at me tentatively and handed me my bouquet. She avoided eye contact. She seemed shy and uncomfortable, as if she were simply doing what she'd been asked. I thanked her in Thai. Everywhere I looked, people were crying, but I was dry-eyed, unprepared for the flood of emotions I was about to feel.

One by one, we made our way toward Dhammananda, who sat in a chair under an awning, waiting to receive us. As was customary, she snipped a lock of each woman's hair. As I knelt down at her feet, suddenly and without warning I began sobbing. The tears streamed down my face. A dam had burst. In that moment I was a child, Dhammananda's love pouring through me. She gently took my hands, and I buried my head in her hands and kissed them. My heart opened, and I felt immense gratitude for her. Dhammananda gently lifted my face up and snipped a single lock of my hair. "Cutting hair is getting rid of the mental defilements," she whispered.

A young Thai woman with short black hair who spoke English quietly approached me. "Are you okay?" Her kindness overwhelmed me. I nodded, though I made little effort to calm my tears. She took my arm and walked with me, helping me find my former place in line. Suddenly, an inner voice spoke to me: *Now you are ready to have your head shaved.* I felt a renewed strength; I released the fear that had held me back and felt a joy unlike anything I had ever known. In that moment, the world shifted, and I began to look through an expanded lens of life steeped in love and understanding.

Thai family members approached me. They were smiling. I understood without speaking that they wanted to clip my hair. I smiled back at them and nodded for them to go ahead. To my surprise I felt elated, as if I were completely free. Soon, all that was left of my hair were a few patches of stubble on my scalp. I walked over to an area where women with electric razors finished shaving my head and eyebrows. I felt clean and pure. We wrapped white kerchiefs around our heads to protect our newly exposed scalps.

I rushed back to my room to look at myself in the mirror. I was not startled to see myself with no hair on my head. What surprised me most were my shaved eyebrows. I hadn't expected that and didn't know about it ahead of time. The reflection in the mirror was a woman I had never seen before. I stood before myself in all my naked presence. All the trappings of my former life vanished. I saw a snowy, eagle-like bird with a sharp beak for a nose, and white-feathered hair tinged with black patches here and there. In that moment, I felt pure inside and out. The black scum of guilt and shame that had been stuck to my insides was gone. My heart blossomed like a lotus flower. I appreciated myself—a quiet, sensitive, intelligent woman with sharply chiseled features.

I called Randall early the next morning. We FaceTimed so he could see what I looked like. At first he was silent. His face was blank, so I couldn't interpret his reaction. Then quietly he said, "Yep, same Cindy on the inside." I felt good about his comment, like he saw through to my true essence. It was a poignant moment shared between us.

The next day was the ordination ceremony. We meditated and chanted together, as we'd done each morning at five thirty. About eight o'clock, we gathered to take our places in line. Dressed in white, we carried three lotus blossoms and walked in procession, circling the Medicine Buddha Vihara three times. Then we gave the lotus blossoms to the bhikkhunis who stood on the lower steps of the vihara.

We entered the Vihara to recite a special prayer. The Thai women had memorized the entire recitation. I had a phonetic transcription of the words in English in order to be able to sound them out. I didn't memorize all the verses since there wasn't time for it. Instead, I concentrated on memorizing two key phrases. The first phrase asked for Dhammananda to protect and take care of me, and the second asked for her forgiveness. Chanting along with the others, I felt rooted in my commitment to be ordained and in my devotion to Dhammananda.

Following the recitation, we bowed one by one before Dhammananda, and walked out of the vihara to a small wooden shed behind the shrine. It was chaotic inside as 124 women struggled to change out of their white clothing into saffron robes. Fortunately, we had the help of temple volunteers, who urged us to change quickly. We had been shown how to fold the *sanghati* (saffron sash), but I was nervous and couldn't get the folds quite right. Luckily, one of the novice nuns came to help me press the layers of fabric together so it draped neatly over my shoulder. Smoothing and patting me down, she adjusted my sash until it was just right.

Once outside, we each received our alms bowls from a trusted family member—in my case, the same Thai woman who had partnered with me earlier. Then we received our ordained name; mine was Dhammanandiya. I later asked Dhammananda to translate the meaning for me. She explained that Dhamma referred to the teachings of the Buddha. Nanda was the name of the princess who was the daughter of Maha Pajapati, the first woman to be ordained in the Buddha's time. Taken together, the name meant "She who takes pleasure in the Dhamma." I was proud of my name; it sounded like Dhammananda only with a different ending. *Like mother, like daughter,* I thought.

This marked the end of the ordination ceremony. Everyone gathered at the front entrance of the temple, smiling, taking pictures, and admiring their new robes as if we were one happy family. I was elated to feel so close to all the Thai women; it was the feeling I'd longed for from the beginning. I trusted my sisters in the Dhamma, shining bright in their new robes.

When I came home, I felt stronger, with a new sense of confidence born from my ordination experience, as if I had undergone a ritual rite of passage and emerged a new woman.

I hadn't realized it at the time, but looking back at the ceremony, the moment I knelt before Dhammananda and started to sob was a life-changing experience. The feelings came on so fast that it was all I could do to make sense of the process. My heart, which had been hardened and closed for so long, cracked open. All my childhood pain and sadness came tumbling out. Dhammananda's profound love had touched me to my core. When she took my hands in hers, it was as if she were ministering a sacred benediction. I felt her warmth and caring like a soft glove against my face. All my life I had wanted my parents' blessing. Dhammananda's unconditional love gave me the permission I had been seeking to let go of my self-hatred and resentment. She was the nurturing mother I had always yearned for.

Over the previous nine years, Dhammananda had been sowing seeds of compassion in my soul, but it was only in that breakthrough moment, when I bowed before my teacher, that I truly understood what she meant. It was the embodiment of an idea that Dhammananda had been laying the groundwork for all along—to learn to love myself. Loving myself helped pave the way to forgiving my mother.

In the month following my ordination, I began to think about my mother's life in context. She didn't appear to have had a close relationship with her own mother, who was older and spoke no English. I had the feeling that my mother, like me, had been left on her own growing up. She'd never told me she felt lonely or neglected as a child, but I had the sense that she never felt loved.

As I came to understand the complexity of my mother, I began to appreciate her for who she was. Part of my healing process had been to quell the angry voices in my head, to open my heart and empathize with my mother's situation. I thought about what Dhammananda said when I first met her: "We cannot solve anything with anger. Anger doesn't lead us anywhere. It is more difficult to practice compassion and loving-kindness. That is the goal of Buddhism."

Dhammananda's love helped me come full circle. If my mother were alive today, I would tell her how much I loved her, how much she inspired me, and how much she meant to me. There are few relationships more important than that between a daughter and her mother. Once that is healed, we gain our birthright as women. Dhammananda allowed me to heal my relationship with my mother, to learn to accept myself, and to become the whole person I was meant to be. I was grateful to Dhammananda, who had so generously taken me into her inner circle and honored my presence with her love and compassion. I carried the love of my teacher as a constant reminder to be true to myself and speak from the heart. I am eternally grateful to Dhammananda and always will be.

As I approach Dhammananda, I begin to cry.
December 5, 2014

Dhammananda reaches toward me to clip the first
lock of hair right before I prepare to have my head shaved.
December 5, 2014

*I am pictured on the left feeling elated right after
being ordained. December 5, 2014*

Epilogue

My most recent visit with Dhammananda was early in 2019 to celebrate the New Year. I returned to the temple, as I had so many times before, to discover myself all over again. My roots were buried deep there. I felt protected, as if sealed off from the outside world, free to explore my rich inner life.

Two weeks before I flew to Bangkok, I emailed Dhammananda to let her know my arrival date and time. I had few expectations for the trip, which felt different for me. On past visits, I had come seeking Dhammananda's advice. I'd relied on her guidance for my internal well-being and happiness. But this time I felt a newly awakened part of myself, less dependent on her and more reliant on myself. It was as if I'd completed the cycle that had begun fourteen years earlier when we'd first met. I felt as if I'd come into the fully embodied presence of my ordained name, Dhammanandiya.

When my plane landed in Bangkok, I caught a cab and headed straight to the temple. Passing through the gates, I felt a sense of relief, like coming home. Several dogs rushed up to me. I looked for Dot Com but didn't see her, nor did I recognize the nun in the front office. *Where's Dhammavanna?* I wondered. The nun handed me a key to my room and said in broken English, "Dhammananda wait for you." My face flushed. Dhammananda had never personally greeted me on arrival. This was new, and I wasn't sure what it meant. Exhausted from the long trip and filled with adrenaline, I left my suitcase in the office and headed down the main path. I was nervous to bow down before her. At sixty-seven, my knees weren't as flexible as in the past. I hoped I could manage it.

I soon spotted her sitting outside in a familiar place where she often met visitors, in a protected area shaded from the sun. Filled with anticipation and praying my knees wouldn't give out, I began to bend down. As I did, she motioned for me to get up. "No, no," she said. "You don't have to bow on the concrete." Thankful, I approached her, reassured by her relaxed manner. "Here, take this one," she said, patting the seat next to her. Her peaceful presence calmed me.

"I'm so glad to see you," I said. Seeing her seated next to me was like a dream. I hadn't seen her in two years. I had imagined this moment so many times in my head that when it actually happened, I wasn't sure what I felt.

We talked briefly and then she said, "Now you go up to the room to rest." I didn't feel ready to leave, but immediately I could see that the next few days would be an opportunity to rekindle our heartfelt connection, no matter how much or how little time I might be able to spend with her one-on-one.

The next day after breakfast, I asked her attendant, whom everyone called Dr. A, if I could meet with Dhammananda. Dr. A approached her on my behalf and then returned to tell me she would meet me at one o'clock. I had several questions to ask in preparation for an article she had asked me to write about my relationship to her as my spiritual teacher. She'd invited me to present my article along with four other speakers at an upcoming conference in June in Nepal. A group of monks in Katmandu were planning a seventy-fifth birthday celebration for her in six months; they were calling it her Diamond Jubilee.

As I'd done in the past, I asked if I could record our conversation, which she agreed to. I asked her to describe whether she had found it difficult with her sons when she returned to Thailand after she was first ordained. The conversation got off to a slow start. She seemed reserved in her responses and gave "stock" replies that I was familiar with from previous interviews. But then, a few minutes into our conversation, things picked up and she grew more animated. Her face brightened and her voice rose with excitement. She fed off my energy, and I fed off hers. The more engaged we became with one another, the more fun we had. Toward the end, her answers became more personal.

I had seen pictures of her posted on Facebook in November and was concerned because I saw that she was sitting in a wheelchair. I knew she had neuropathy in her feet and was worried she was in pain. "How is your health?" I inquired.

"I've slowed down," she replied. She said that the pain in her feet had worsened over time. That explained the wheelchair. I imagined it was painful to walk too far. I asked if she was traveling much, and she said she would travel to Nepal, India, and China, but no longer wanted to take long international flights as she had when she was younger.

"I only go to places where people want me," she said. I took this to mean she only accepted invitations to speak where the audience embraced her position supporting women's ordination.

At seventy-four, I could see she was more reserved. Her back slumped slightly, which it had never done before. She told me that she was assigning some of her responsibilities to the other nuns. Whereas she used to make arrangements for all visitors who wanted to stay at the temple, now Venerable Dhammaparipunna, one of the nuns who spoke English, dealt with guests. Then she surprised me when she added, "I'm ready to go now. I've done what I came to do." We'd never broached that subject of her dying before. I hadn't considered it and wasn't ready to think about it there and then. It could be in part because it reminded me of my mother's death, which I hadn't thought about in a long time.

It only took a moment for me to drift back in time to recall the last two weeks of my mother's life. Everything about her had softened as death grew near. It was as if she accepted her vulnerability and the inevitability of her death, but spoke not a word about it to me. She would just look at me with trusting eyes as if to acknowledge, *We know what's coming and thanks for being here.* I never remember her saying thank you out loud, but she conveyed that message with a kind look of affection in her eyes.

At ninety, she had a dignity about her that lasted right up to her death. She never said "I want to die"—she simply stopped eating. Her silent declaration said to me, *It's time.* She was peaceful when the hospice nurse was called in. A diabetic since age sixty-five, she had decided to stop taking her insulin. After three days she slipped into a coma. No one knew how long it would be until she died. I remembered thinking it could happen anytime, and that I wanted to be there so that she wouldn't be alone. On day five I lay down on the carpeted floor of her apartment next to her hospital bed. All the nurses had gone for a while, so I didn't feel self-conscious about lying down. I wanted to help my mother let go. I closed my eyes and propped my knees up. I'm not sure where the image came from but I visualized her mother, Hannah Esther Pearlman, above her bed, beckoning for my mother to join her.

"Look," I whispered. "Your mother is here to welcome you to the other side. Don't be afraid. It's safe now; you can let go." I felt a childlike sense of wonder that I could help her release from this life.

I left at eleven that night and asked the hospice nurse to call me if there was any sudden change. At home, tired after a long day, I fell asleep. The phone woke me at four o'clock. I picked it up, still groggy from sleep. A woman's voice said, "Your mother passed twenty minutes ago." I felt a rush of emotions all at once. I was angry that the nurse hadn't called me earlier, disappointed because I wanted to be with my mom, and saddened that she was really gone.

When I looked back on my mother's death and the way it happened, I realized that she died exactly the way she wanted. She came into this world determined to live life on her own terms, and she departed on her own terms. She had a dignified death, and I was proud of her.

Suspended in my thoughts, my focus slowly came back into the room. I looked down at my recording device and noticed we'd been talking for an hour. I switched off the recorder. Dhammananda began asking about me: "How are you doing? How are things for you at home?" I told her I was genuinely happy and doing well. I remembered all the times I had come to visit, relying on her to help me resolve personal problems, but now that I was stronger, our relationship was changing. I no longer needed her to take care of me. I simply wanted to spend time with her and enjoy her company.

That night I dreamed about Dhammananda. In the dream she was tired. I helped her into bed to lie down and covered her with a blanket. I woke up thinking about what the dream meant. Perhaps it was my way of accepting the fact that she was aging, and our roles were shifting. Sooner rather than later, she might need my help. I imagined sitting by her side, chatting and keeping her company. I wanted to be able to support her emotionally in the same way she had supported me.

In the next few days we talked only briefly. She'd come up to me after breakfast to offer a slice of cake or some fruit from the buffet. I was at peace with our minimal contact in a way I wouldn't have been before. I used to crave her personal attention, but now I was content to immerse myself in the daily activities of the temple. As always, I rose at five to prepare for morning chanting. During the day, I volunteered for odd jobs, like cleaning out the fountains where scum had collected, making paper beads to string across the entrance to Dhammananda's office door, or cleaning the third floor of the main vihara—anything that needed to be done. Late in the afternoon, I worked in the garden during "community" time and, around seven o'clock, joined the nuns for evening chanting.

After seven days, the rigors of temple life were starting to wear on me—taking cold showers, waking before dawn, and sleeping on a two-inch mattress. On day eight of my visit, I reminded Dhammananda that I would be leaving in two days. We chatted for a few minutes in her office, but I could see she was busy working. After about five minutes, I excused myself so that she could get back to her work.

The next day she came up to me after breakfast and told me to meet her at one o'clock. "We will go to see a wax museum nearby," she said. This came as a surprise to me, and I was grateful to spend personal time with her.

Promptly at one, Dr. A pulled her black sedan up next to the office. She had short clipped black hair and a serious demeanor. Completely dedicated to Dhammananda, she ministered to her every need. I had seen Dhammananda lean on her assistant's arm after evening chanting. Dr. A would gently guide her into the elevator to take her down to the first floor. She drove Dhammananda to doctor's appointments and arranged for all her medical needs.

As I looked inside the car, I saw Dhammananda sitting in the back seat. I thought it was strange for me to take the front seat but didn't question it. Later in passing conversation, Dr. A said that Dhammananda was more comfortable resting in the back while she drove.

Dhammananda liked to take short trips away from the temple. In her role as abbess, everyone depended on her to make decisions. Getting away gave her a chance to leave all her responsibilities behind. As the car sped down the highway, Dhammananda's mood brightened. She even rested her bare foot on the divider between the two front seats and wiggled her toes, nudging Dr. A slightly. She took on the aura of a much younger person, curious and delighted to explore her surroundings.

When we arrived at the museum entrance, Dr. A asked Dhammananda if she would like a wheelchair. She welcomed the suggestion, and I pushed her wheelchair as we strolled down pathways surrounded by lush green plants. It was heavier than I imagined and swiveled slightly as I guided it forward, but I was pleased to be able to take care of her in this small way. The air was cool and pleasant for walking, not too hot.

The first building we encountered was dedicated to the history of the Thai royal family. There were stairs leading up to the main entrance, so Dhammananda said she would prefer to wait outside for us. I felt funny leaving her behind, but Dr. A was apparently used to this and wheeled her into a shady spot to rest while we were inside. We spent about twenty minutes touring the exhibit, and when we returned, Dhammananda was sitting patiently observing the scenery.

Mid-afternoon we stopped for a drink. Dhammananda

ordered tea. When it was served, she said in a playful way, "I don't like Earl Grey tea, and they don't have milk." Then she laughed. "I just want to complain." She talked about her grandchildren, how much they would like the exhibit. I could see that family was very important to her. This was a private side of Dhammananda that I hadn't heard her mention before. Perhaps now that she was older, she wanted to be closer to them. As we sipped our drinks and relaxed, we watched a nearby waterfall that made soft percussive sounds tapping on the surface below. The whole afternoon felt like an adventure; there was no pressure. We were there for the simple pleasure of spending time together and enjoying ourselves.

On the ride back to the temple, Dhammananda suggested that Dr. A take me out to dinner that evening. I felt like she was taking special care of me. After a week of eating basic soup, vegetables, and rice, I looked forward to an evening meal at a restaurant. After a short rest back at the temple, Dr. A retrieved me and took me to the central town of Nakon Pathom, which was about a ten-minute drive from the temple. We pulled up to a street-side restaurant with outdoor tables and chairs.

"You're going to love this food," she said. She ordered several tofu dishes and a papaya salad. Each flavorful forkful melted in my mouth.

During the meal, our conversation turned to our concerns about Dhammananda. We both worried that she was still taking on too much and needed to slow down. Thinking of Dhammananda's earlier comment, I asked Dr. A who would take over when she passed on. "No one," she said, "could replace Dhammananda." She referred to her as an "historic figure" in bringing about change, a "trailblazer." She called her the Abraham Lincoln of her time. I wasn't quite sure how Dr. A drew the analogy to Lincoln but inferred that it had to do with how Dhammananda had freed Thai women to live out their full potential as spiritual beings.

Dr. A planned to be ordained once Dhammananda was gone and said the temple would continue to be managed by a committee of bhikkhuni who would share in the responsibilities of running it. I couldn't imagine the temple without Dhammananda and wondered if I would want to visit once she was no longer there. All these thoughts drifted in and out of my head as we finished eating. The whole meal came to the equivalent of fifteen dollars. I was stuffed and thanked Dr. A as we pulled back through the temple gates. We had missed the seven o'clock chanting, so I simply returned to my room for the evening. *What an incredible day,* I thought. *So many wonderful experiences.* I was glowing inside.

The next morning I planned to leave the temple at eight-thirty to catch a morning flight to southern Thailand, where I planned to stay at a beach resort in Khao Lak for a few days. I wanted to see how the community had changed in the years following the tsunami. I woke early for morning prayers and had breakfast. When I finished eating, I looked over to Dhammananda and knew it was time to say goodbye. I didn't expect her to say much, since in the past our goodbyes had been fairly straightforward.

I approached her table and knelt down. When I told her I was leaving, I heard her whisper, "Come closer." As I leaned in toward her she wrapped her arms around me and hugged me. I felt her soft body beneath the robes as I pressed my chest against her breast. A fluid, warm feeling swept over me. As we held onto one another's arms, I looked directly into her eyes and said, "I love you." As we slowly let go, tears streamed down my cheeks. I stood up and took one final bow. I felt a sense of completion, as if our love were sealed forever.

I had a strange feeling as I walked away. I felt as though she were giving me a final goodbye. It may have occurred to her that, no matter what happened, there was closure. I had arrived at the place where she wanted me to be and where I wanted to be. Dhammananda had given me the blessing of her maternal love, and it touched me deeply. My healing journey was now complete.

As I reflected back on that moment we shared, I realized how touching it was in so many ways. It is unusual for an ordained person to touch someone, much less hug them. On the way to the airport, I thought about my own mother. I had never experienced such physical closeness with her. I do remember hugging her, but her body always seemed stiff, as if she couldn't quite let me in or reciprocate my love.

I considered my journey and the possibility that had been opened to me to heal my maternal wounds. The potential is there for any woman to heal old wounds that bind her, but she must be willing, have courage, and be lucky enough to find a wise teacher who is capable of loving and accepting her just as she is. I came to understand this truth over time. When we go forward with a truly open heart, faith, forgiveness, and love are possible.

Dhammananda and I are standing near the temple entrance in June 2017. You can see the Chinese Buddha seated at the front gate to Songdhammakalyani Temple in the background.

Prayer for Dhammananda:

Three deep bows to Venerable Dhammananda Bhikkhuni. Venerable Mother, you gave me my life back. You have helped me heal and become the woman I am meant to be. You made my heart whole. Words cannot express how grateful I am to you for taking me under your wing. Your prophetic words of advice are an inspiration to me, a light out of the darkness. And I am not alone. You are a pillar of strength and a beacon of hope for so many women and men whose lives you have changed forever. *Sadhu. Sadhu. Sadhu.*

Acknowledgments

Writing this book has been a journey of the heart and I have many people to thank who accompanied me on the path.

Let me begin by thanking my "Willful" Sisters, whose inspiration provided me the encouragement and validation I needed to continue writing. Anne Woods, Ellie Wood, Mary Brent Cantarutti, Catherine Pyke, Adrienne Amundsen, and Gail Strickland thank you for your unwavering support.

My deepest thanks go to Brooke Warner publisher of She Writes Press and my editor, whose sage advice guided me word by word. You urged me to continue and nurtured me along even when I had no idea where I was headed. Thanks for believing in me.

I want to acknowledge Nancy Zarider for her beautiful photographs and for her enduring friendship.

Deepest gratitude goes to my family. To Randall Rasicot for his love and support, and to Kristopher Antoni Rasicot, your smile lights up my day.

I am particularly grateful to Marilee Stark, who has accompanied me on my journey and provided me the sacred space to blossom. I treasure our time together.

Kathryn Pearlman Levy, my mother, thank you for your strength, courage, and conviction. Your dreams are my inspiration.

About the Author

Cindy Rasicot's life has been a spiritual journey since she was a small child. At four she asked her older brother (who was five at the time): "Where is God?" His answer: "Everywhere." Puzzled, she looked all around her, but didn't find evidence. She kept her brother's words in her heart while growing up, and figured she'd have an answer someday. In the meantime, she got her master's degree in marriage, family, and child counseling, married, and held management positions in non-profits for twenty-five years—all while exploring her passion for dance, art, and writing.

Cindy's spiritual journey took on new dimensions when she, her husband, and their son moved to Bangkok, Thailand for three years. She met her spiritual teacher, Venerable Dhammananda Bhikkuni, the first fully ordained Thai Theravada nun—an encounter that opened her heart and changed her life forever. This deepening relationship led to writing her memoir, *Finding Venerable Mother: A Daughter's Spiritual Quest to Thailand,* which chronicles her adventures along the spiritual path.

Her other writings include an article in *Sawasdee Magazine* in 2007 and essays featured in two anthologies: *Wandering in Paris: Luminaries and Love in the City of Light* (Wanderland Writers, 2013) and *A Café in Space: The Anaïs Nin Literary Journal, Volume 11* (Sky Blue Press, 2014). She currently resides in Point Richmond, California, where she writes and enjoys views of the San Francisco Bay. Visit Cindy at www.cindyrasicot.com.

Author photo © Anita Scharf

SELECTED TITLES FROM SHE WRITES PRESS

She Writes Press is an independent publishing company founded to serve women writers everywhere. Visit us at www.shewritespress.com.

Learning to Eat Along the Way by Margaret Bendet. $16.95, 978-1-63152-997-9. After interviewing an Indian holy man, newspaper reporter Margaret Bendet follows him in pursuit of enlightenment and ends up facing demons that were inside her all along.

Motherlines: Letters of Love, Longing, and Liberation by Patricia Reis. $16.95, 978-1-63152-121-8. In her midlife search for meaning, and longing for maternal connection, Patricia Reis encounters uncommon women who inspire her journey and discovers an unlikely confidante in her aunt, a free-spirited Franciscan nun.

This Trip Will Change Your Life: A Shaman's Story of Spirit Evolution by Jennifer B. Monahan. $16.95, 978-1-63152-111-9. One woman's inspirational story of finding her life purpose and the messages and training she received from the spirit world as she became a shamanic healer.

Raw by Bella Mahaya Carter. $16.95, 978-1-63152-345-8. In an effort to holistically cure her chronic stomach problems, Bella Mahaya Carter adopted a 100 percent raw, vegan diet—a first step on a quest that ultimately dragged her, kicking and screaming, into spiritual adulthood.

Godmother: An Unexpected Journey, Perfect Timing, and Small Miracles by Odile Atthalin. $16.95, 978-1-63152-172-0. After thirty years of traveling the world, Odile Atthalin—a French intellectual from a well-to-do family in Paris—ends up in Berkeley, CA, where synchronicities abound and ultimately give her everything she has been looking for, including the gift of becoming a godmother.

Not a Poster Child: Living Well with a Disability–A Memoir by Francine Falk-Allen. $16.95, 978-1631523915. Francine Falk-Allen was only three years old when she contracted polio and temporarily lost the ability to stand and walk. Here, she tells the story of how a toddler learned grown-up lessons too soon; a schoolgirl tried her best to be a "normie," on into young adulthood; and a woman finally found her balance, physically and spiritually.